101 WAYS

to Make **Studying** Easier and Faster for

College

Students

*What Every Student Needs to Know
Explained Simply*

By Susan M. Roubidoux

101 WAYS TO MAKE STUDYING EASIER AND FASTER FOR COLLEGE STUDENTS: WHAT EVERY STUDENT NEEDS TO KNOW EXPLAINED SIMPLY

Copyright © 2008 by Atlantic Publishing Group, Inc.
1405 SW 6th Ave. • Ocala, Florida 34471 • 800-814-1132 • 352-622-1875–Fax
Web site: www.atlantic-pub.com • E-mail: sales@atlantic-pub.com
SAN Number: 268-1250

ISBN-13: 978-1-60138-249-8   ISBN-10: 1-60138-249-9

Library of Congress Cataloging-in-Publication Data

Roubidoux, Susan Marie, 1976-
   101 ways to make studying easier and faster for college students : what every student needs to know explained simply / Susan Marie Roubidoux.
      p. cm.
   Includes bibliographical references and index.
   ISBN-13: 978-1-60138-249-8 (alk. paper)
   ISBN-10: 1-60138-249-9 (alk. paper)
   1. Study skills--United States. 2. College student orientation--United States. 3. Active learning--United States. I. Title. II. Title: One hundred one ways to make studying easier and faster for college students.

   LB2395.R76 2008
   371.3'028'1--dc22
                              2008010795

Printed on Recycled Paper

INTERIOR LAYOUT DESIGN: Vickie Taylor • vtaylor@atlantic-pub.com

Printed in the United States

We recently lost our beloved pet "Bear," who was not only our best and dearest friend but also the "Vice President of Sunshine" here at Atlantic Publishing. He did not receive a salary but worked tirelessly 24 hours a day to please his parents. Bear was a rescue dog that turned around and showered myself, my wife Sherri, his grandparents Jean, Bob and Nancy and every person and animal he met (maybe not rabbits) with friendship and love. He made a lot of people smile every day.

We wanted you to know that a portion of the profits of this book will be donated to The Humane Society of the United States. *–Douglas & Sherri Brown*

The human-animal bond is as old as human history. We cherish our animal companions for their unconditional affection and acceptance. We feel a thrill when we glimpse wild creatures in their natural habitat or in our own backyard.

Unfortunately, the human-animal bond has at times been weakened. Humans have exploited some animal species to the point of extinction.

The Humane Society of the United States makes a difference in the lives of animals here at home and worldwide. The HSUS is dedicated to creating a world where our relationship with animals is guided by compassion. We seek a truly humane society in which animals are respected for their intrinsic value, and where the human-animal bond is strong.

Want to help animals? We have plenty of suggestions. Adopt a pet from a local shelter, join The Humane Society and be a part of our work to help companion animals and wildlife. You will be funding our educational, legislative, investigative and outreach projects in the U.S. and across the globe.

Or perhaps you'd like to make a memorial donation in honor of a pet, friend or relative? You can through our Kindred Spirits program. And if you'd like to contribute in a more structured way, our Planned Giving Office has suggestions about estate planning, annuities, and even gifts of stock that avoid capital gains taxes.

Maybe you have land that you would like to preserve as a lasting habitat for wildlife. Our Wildlife Land Trust can help you. Perhaps the land you want to share is a backyard— that's enough. Our Urban Wildlife Sanctuary Program will show you how to create a habitat for your wild neighbors.

So you see, it's easy to help animals. And The HSUS is here to help.

THE HUMANE SOCIETY
OF THE UNITED STATES.

2100 L Street NW • Washington, DC 20037 • 202-452-1100

www.hsus.org

TABLE OF CONTENTS

PREFACE

Most college graduates fall into one of three categories. The first group is those who spent all of their college years studying and had little time for fun or extracurricular activities. They graduated with honors and had tremendous academic success but did not seem to have time to have much fun or social interaction while in college. The second group is those who spent the majority of their college years partying, slacking off, and barely making the grades they needed to graduate and get a decent job. The third group is those who were able to do well in class and still have fun and get the "life" education that is almost as important as the degree. They may have graduated with honors and they were successful in many facets of their education including extracurricular activities.

Students who are able to find the balance between academic and social activities make the most of their college years and will look back with fond memories of what they learned and how they learned it. The social activities — whether it is regularly taking one or two nights a week to hang out with friends, involvement in extracurricular activities, or both – help the students develop an independence and self-actualization that can rarely be found elsewhere. This is the time in their lives when they start to decide what is important; if they spend all of their time studying and preparing for class they will not have the opportunities to make these decisions. In addition, the material they are learning in class is also the basis for the same decisions.

A book about studying and success in college is not complete without discussing ways students can make the most of their time there. This book does just that. It explains the skills students need to make the most of their college years from time management, organization, and specific studying strategies to taking advantage of all the college or university has to offer in terms of extra activities and learning opportunities.

INTRODUCTION

I t is a typical scene. New college students have done all of the necessary preparations, from taking exams to filling out applications to registering for classes. If they are fresh out of high school, they have likely settled into a residence hall and met their new roommates. If they are non-traditional students, they have made arrangements with their "other life" to fit in the scheduled classes. However, their preparations are not complete.

New college students anticipate and prepare for many of the changes and challenges they will face in this new chapter in their lives, but they may overlook the challenges that brought them to college in the first place. College is about growing, changing, and having fun, but it is also about learning, studying, and succeeding in class. New college students forget classes and studying in college are so completely different than what they became accustomed to in high school and other areas of their lives.

According to the *U.S. News & World Report* article "Get In, Show Up, Drop Out: Trying to Learn Why So Many College Students Fail to Graduate," author Alex Kingsbury reports statistics showing that only 63 percent of students who enter four-year colleges have their degrees within six years. Kingsbury explains that the main focus of both lawmakers and teachers is to get students accepted to college, but they do not do much to prepare them for college.

Students fail because college is difficult and because it is a different playing field than their previous educational experiences. Statistics show that even the most successful high school students can have a difficult time when it comes to succeeding in college. The most intelligent student can fail.

The reason for this is twofold. First, for many people studying is not a natural talent. It is something that needs to be learned and practiced to be successful. Furthermore, the study skills and techniques necessary to succeed in high school are different than those needed in college. This is not to say that college students need to forget their previous methods of studying; they just need to be willing to build on and expand what they already know to adapt to this new environment. The second reason intelligent students fail is new college students have a skewed idea of what college will be like and are not prepared. Because of this surprise, they are overwhelmed by the expectations and go from one extreme or the other. Some spend all of their time studying, which can lead them to burn out quickly, while others try to get by without making any adjustments and end up skimming through college without getting the most from their experience.

OBSTACLES FACING COLLEGE STUDENTS

New college students face a myriad of obstacles. Here is a closer look at the obstacles contributing to why students fail in college:

- **Class Structure**. In high school, classes meet every day so students have frequent contact with teachers and have time for a variety of activities including study sessions and workdays; they have opportunities to get direct help from their teachers. In college, however, classes may meet only two or three times per week. The time in class is usually dedicated to lecture, discussion, and other direct learning activities. Work and study sessions, including a fairly heavy load of reading, must take place outside of class. A class grade may rely on a few activities, projects, or tests, so the "in-between" things (such as reading assignments, discussion questions, and quizzes) go ungraded. This is a difficult transition for students who expect to receive feedback on every assignment, and it makes it easy for students to lose motivation or skip an assignment because "no one will know."

Student Schedule. In high school, the schedule was jam-packed all day long with classes and possibly a study hall. Students had their evenings to get their work done and participate in other activities. In college, it is likely students will have classes scheduled throughout the day with breaks in between and differing schedules from one day to the next. Regardless of which schedule they prefer, having their schedules dictated to them in high school and then coming to a place where they are responsible for how they spend their time is often a difficult phase for new college students.

Expectations. Professor and instructor expectations of college students take a huge jump from what high school teachers expect. College students are expected to do a large percentage of work independently and outside of class, and test material is not always covered in class. Professors try to elicit a higher level of critical thinking and problem solving from their students, which can take more time and more mental effort than high school classes.

Distractions. Possibly the number one reason students struggle with their studies is distractions. There are new friends to get to know, new events to attend, and new places to see. Pairing this with the newfound freedom of being out on their own can result in a difficult transition to good study habits for students. Non-traditional students face different distractions that can be more demanding on their time, including jobs and family responsibilities. Also, college students may not take advantage of the time between classes. There may be a desire to waste this time because "it is only an hour." Add all these small time increments up over the course of a week, however, and it is time that could have been put to better use.

CHARACTERISTICS OF SUCCESSFUL COLLEGE STUDENTS

In a society where college graduates earn more throughout their lifetimes than those who do not graduate, it is imperative that new college students learn how to be a successful student. Because of all these changes, studying and study skills in college are not simply learning how to take notes and memorize facts. Successful studying for a college student encompasses a lifestyle designed for the individual and by the individual to make sure he or she has a unique, well-rounded college education.

Even though each student is an individual with a unique learning style, there are characteristics apparent in successful college students. They are:

- **Proactive Learning.** Simply reading information to get a sense of what will be on an exam or quiz is not enough to meet and beat the expectations set forth in a college course. Proactive learners are those who take the initiative to read, write, think, and talk about the subject so they get to know and understand the subject matter instead of only memorizing facts.

- **Self Awareness.** Successful college students have a high level of self- awareness when it comes to studying. This includes which subjects they are good at, the times of day they study best, and the techniques and skills they need to succeed. Successful college students also have a myriad of learning strategies available to them so they can pick the one that best fits a specific assignment.

Motivation. It takes motivation to keep going when college life becomes stressful. This means regularly attending class, keeping up with assigned reading, and putting in the hard work necessary to succeed. Students who do what needs to be done on their own probably have the drive and desire it takes to be successful in college.

College students do not naturally have these characteristics. These are learned skills. This book covers the tips and tricks necessary to teach active learning strategies, to promote self-awareness, and to foster motivation.

HOW TO USE THIS BOOK

The goal of this book is to teach college students how to manage their time and master skills to help them study efficiently so they have the opportunity to enjoy college, not just endure it. This book is also a tool to help college students adapt to a new and more demanding learning environment. It tries to show college students that being successful in college is much more than getting an "A" — more reason than ever for students to learn how to study quickly and efficiently so they have time for all of the extra opportunities they want to take advantage of while in college.

Each student has individual needs and reasons for reading this book. It is designed for easy access to the areas of greatest concern. A good way to start is to read the entire book. This will start the journey with an overview of the tips to having a successful and enjoyable college experience. After an initial reading, the book can be used as a point-by-point resource to help stay on track and refresh skills in whatever areas are lacking. For example, if someone wants to find help in time management, they can read and implement the strategies in that section to help improve their success.

Throughout the book are case studies with tips and commentary from students, professors, administrators, and other experts. Do not be afraid to try their tips and tricks. They worked for someone else and they just might work again.

Part 1

SETTING YOURSELF UP FOR SUCCESS:

WHAT TO DO NOW

Studying does not come naturally; it is a learned process that takes time and organization. To be successful, it is important to set the scene to help make studying more accessible and to remove all the possible reasons for avoiding studying or shoving it aside for something else. Procrastination leads to problems such as cramming for a test in middle of the night or skipping a class to finish work for another. Getting these issues under control is the first step toward seeing results as a successful student.

MAKE A SCHEDULE

Time management is a dirty word to many people. The thought of designing and following a strict schedule is mind-boggling and confining. However, a successful student knows that a schedule can help the busiest student stay on top of what needs to be done and have time to relax, unwind, and have fun without stressing about what still needs to be done for class tomorrow, the next day, or next week. This is possible because proper time management gives every class, task, and assignment — as well as downtime — its own timeslot.

It may take a little practice, but a schedule can help successful students fit in time with friends, a regular workout, and a study break to watch a favorite television show without feeling guilty about not studying or working on an assignment, all without compromising their grades.

Here are some signs that a student needs to have a schedule:

- The student is constantly cramming for exams and writing papers or completing projects at the last minute.

- The student has to skip one class to finish the work for another class.

- The student attends class but spends the time working and studying for another class.

- The student is frequently multi-tasking to try to get everything done.

- The student is constantly having to make decisions between fun and work and feeling guilty either way.

- The student is pulling all-nighters.

DETERMINE WHERE TIME GOES

Before sitting down and writing a schedule it is helpful to determine how a student's time is used each day. To do this, students should spend a few days keeping track of what they do all day from the minute they wake up until they go to bed. This will help illustrate what parts of the day are important to keep in the schedule and what parts are wasted time.

Students will be surprised how much time each day is wasted. It does not seem like much when it comes in 10- or 20-minute increments, but it can add up quickly. One of the greatest benefits of time tracking is it shows the student how much time they have during the week. If this time is used efficiently, it can make for more enjoyable "free" time. Another benefit of determining how time is spent is seeing what incidentals are important to the student so he or she knows when and how to schedule their activities.

Here are some examples of information that may be discovered when tracking how time is spent:

- One student may determine he needs an hour in the morning to wake up, have breakfast, and get ready for the day. This is something that should take priority on the schedule.

- Another student may find trying to squeeze in studying between her afternoon classes does not work because she gets distracted and ends up daydreaming. This is an indication that the time slot should be used for something else. It may be a good time for a break so she can do something she enjoys.

- Yet another student may realize going to study in the student union is a waste of time because even though he is there for three hours every afternoon, he spends 75 minutes of the time talking.

- Another student may realize even though she spends an hour and a half at the cafeteria almost every night for dinner, she and her friends have good discussions that revitalize to study more. She used to feel guilty about taking that break, but she now realizes it is too important to cut out of her day.

DETERMINE THE BEST STUDY TIME

People have certain times of the day when they are better able to concentrate. It is important for students to determine when these times are so they can add study blocks into their schedule at times that will lead to successful studying.

The best way to determine this time is to evaluate the time spent studying at different times of the day and make a note of the most and least efficient times. This may change from day to day, depending on each day's schedule. Some students may have two morning classes right away and then be able to study midmorning until lunch three days a week, but on the other two days, they may have two particularly difficult and draining classes in the morning so the midmorning study sessions are not productive.

While this is an individual determination and may change from semester to semester depending on the class load and schedule, successful students find they are best able to work between breakfast and dinner. After dinner may be a time of socialization, and it is when the body begins to wind down from the day. Granted this is not true for everyone, but those who can find the time to study and work before dinner and have their evenings open for relaxation tend to be rejuvenated and ready when they wake up the next morning.

Other considerations to remember when determining the best study times:

- Studying late at night across campus is not the best choice for someone who does not want to walk home alone.

- Some study spots are in buildings that close during certain hours so they cannot be relied on throughout the day.

- Job schedules may not be consistent, so students may have to be willing to shuffle study times around depending on their schedules.

- Long classes, such as three- or four-hour night classes, can be draining; successful students do not plan on any heavy studying after this time.

- Considering when friends and roommates have free time is also important. For example, students find that if all of their friends keep Saturday afternoons open for fun activities, they are less likely to want to study and more likely to cancel a study session at the last minute for something fun. Successful students take these things into consideration when making their schedules so they can still enjoy social activities with their friends.

SET UP A REGULAR SCHEDULE

Instead of setting up a schedule that has time slots indicated on the hour, make up a schedule template that follows the university's class schedule. So if classes go from 8 to 9, 9:10 to 10:10, 10:20 to 11:20, 11:30 to 12:30, and so on, this is how the successful student's schedule should look on paper. Colleges and university schedules are typically different Monday-Wednesday-Friday than Tuesday-Thursday, so weekly schedules should reflect the differences.

When setting up a schedule it is important to add items whose times are set such as classes, meetings, jobs, and anything else considered important enough to write into the schedule, such as a weekly dinner at a relative's house or a yoga class two times a week. It is also important to schedule times for fun and relaxation. Some successful students like to take Sunday afternoon, for example, and not schedule anything else. Others like to have one to two hours of downtime each night.

Next, schedule study blocks. On average, successful students plan to spend two hours studying per week for every hour per week spent in class. However, some classes may require more time, and students who tend to read more slowly should figure in more time as well.

Here are things to consider when planning which items need to go into the regular schedule:

- **Successful students** start with their classes and schedule everything else around these times.

- **Successful students** use their schedules to make the most of their time between classes. Often there is not enough time to go home and get back to campus in time for the next class, so it is important to figure out how to use this time efficiently.

- **Successful students** recognize the importance of relaxation and taking the time to stay healthy, including exercising and eating right.

- **Successful students** often want to get more out of college than just a degree, so they join at least one club or organization and make a point to attend meetings and other functions, so these items also appear in the schedule.

- **Successful students** know when their professors have office hours so they can stop in when they need to ask a question. While these are not listed as time commitments on the schedule, they can be notated so they are easily accessible when needed.

- **Successful students** also take the time to know when the labs are available for student use. Again, these are not listed on the schedule as commitments, but they should be notated so that when the services are needed, the student does not need to waste time scrambling to see when they are open.

COMMIT TO GOING TO EVERY CLASS

Successful students go to class. Professors say the number one thing students do to harm their grades is skip class. Even if the class does not have penalties for missing, the student suffers by not attending and keeping up with the information. Class periods offer valuable discussion or information that cannot be replicated by copying someone's notes or reading the textbook or other materials required for the class.

Students who attend class and stick to their schedules are more likely to use their time during the day wisely. Skipping a morning class to sleep in sets the student up to have a rushed, stressed, and "off" day because they have not stuck to their normal routine.

Professors like to see their students attend class. Here are some other benefits of attending class:

- **Successful students** know they get a more thorough and internalized understanding of the subject when they are exposed to it on a regular basis.

- **Successful students** get more out of class when they participate in the discussions and class activities led by the professor.

- **Successful students** can take advantage of the time immediately following class to ask the professor questions.

- **Successful students** get to know their professors by attending class. Knowing their professors can help them, anticipate how they will grade, and what types of questions may be asked on an exam.

- **Successful students** get to know their professors, so professors may be more understanding if the student is struggling with concepts in the class or if the student has an emergency and needs to miss class or make up an exam or assignment.

- **Successful students** avoid grade penalties from unexcused absences by attending all of their classes.

PLAN STUDY BLOCKS

Putting time in the schedule for studying is important, but long blocks of time set aside for studying can be daunting. Here are some tips:

- **Take breaks.** Successful students might study for 50 minutes and then take a 10 minute break: go for a walk, have a snack, chat with friends, check e-mail, or stretch and take a bathroom break.

- **Change it up.** After a break, successful students change subjects or tasks. Reading the same textbook for hours on end is not effective.

- **Plan ahead.** Successful students bring all the supplies and materials needed for the assignment or project at hand.

- **Set priorities.** Successful students put their most difficult assignments at the top of the list for each study block so they can tackle these when their brains are fresh.

Compensate for Special Circumstances

No time management plan will work without allowing room for extenuating circumstances. There will be weeks when students have several exams and papers due. These weeks will require more studying than other weeks. This is when students have to give up some of the "fun" activities. This may mean skipping dinner with friends and packing food to eat on a study break, taping their favorite show, or missing a workout. It may also mean having to study outside their ideal study times. Occasionally, this higher degree of intensity is necessary, but successful students have the foundation in place to get through without a complete disruption of their lives.

There are also times when the best intentions go awry. Students get sick and have emergencies that make keeping scheduled study sessions impossible for a day or two. Friends, phone calls, and other distractions take over. It happens to all students at one time or another. The key is to minimize these occurrences and to rearrange other free time to make up for it.

Here are some other special circumstances that may cause a glitch in the schedule:

- A friend has an emergency and needs help.

- A boss has requested all employees work more hours during a busy week.

- A professor announces a mistake in the syllabus which adds an assignment or changes the scope of a project.

- A member of a group project is not pulling his or her weight leaving the other members to pick up slack.

- A student is feeling the effects of the stress and decides to take a "mental health day."

- A special event such as a concert, show, or club activity takes precedence over studying one evening.

One way to stay on top of weeks that have an extra workload due to multiple assignments, projects, or exams is to plan ahead. At the beginning of each semester, successful students take all of their syllabi and write the due dates for all assignments, exams, and projects on their schedules so they can see what is due at a glance.

MAKE TIME FOR FUN

It is easy for college students to get burned out quickly. This is why all college students need to make time for fun.

Using a schedule to help the student visualize where the time is going and how it is being used may give the student the time needed to join an intramural league or a club. It is important for students to remember there is more to college than classes. The extras and the socializing are as important in helping the student learn and grow during this time – as long as it is all kept in balance.

Successful students understand that succeeding in college is more than getting the "A." While getting the grade is important, so are the other social activities that can be as much a learning experience as the 8 a.m. lecture or the afternoon lab.

Colleges and universities offer a variety of social activities and events for their students. Here are ideas on what to do for fun without leaving campus:

- **Join academic** groups. Departments at the university may have discipline-related clubs and organizations. Students can also find honor societies and competition-based teams as well.

- **Join a social organization.** These clubs and organizations are not necessarily affiliated with a discipline on campus but appeal to leisure activities such as the outdoor club, the poetry club, or the film society.

- **Use the university's resources.** This includes art and history galleries, planetariums, theaters, and volunteer organizations.

- **Enjoy the student union.** Student unions offer a variety of entertainment activities including performers, such as speakers, comedians, and musicians.

- **Try something new.** The organizations on college and university campuses like to expose students to new things, such as an a cappella group, an independent film series, or political and social topics speakers.

Students can keep informed about social happenings on campus by reading the official publications, watching the information boards in the student union, and asking what other people in their classes plan on doing. On the same note, when students join organizations, they can help spread the word about these events to help their fellow students find fun activities to attend.

MAKE THE MOST OF TIME BETWEEN CLASSES

The 10 to 15 minutes before classes is a good time to fit in little things that may go undone or become much larger if ignored.

Students with schedules know what needs to be done in the grand scheme of things, but days get hectic for everyone, so the little things can go unnoticed. This is why successful students take a minute or two each night to jot down a list of things that need to be done the next day. It may include returning a library book, meeting with a study group, appearing for an appointment in the financial aid office, or picking up a course schedule for the following year. It could also be a reminder to finish an assignment that did not get done the day before. This way, when students have a spare few minutes, they know what needs to be done.

THINGS STUDENTS CAN DO IN THIS TIME

- **Make a phone call.** This is an opportunity to call someone and set up a time to meet later in the week or month without worrying about being stuck on the phone.

- **Check e-mail.** Even the best intentions of quickly checking e-mail can turn into an hour online. Doing it before the next class allows for a quick check and a few quick replies.

- **See a professor.** If the professor's office is nearby, students can stop in to ask a question. If the answer will take longer than the time available, there will still be time to set up an appointment. At minimum this can set up the basis for an e-mail conversation and it is a way for students to introduce themselves to their professors, especially in large classes.

- **Get some fresh air.** Just going outside to walk around the building before the next class starts can help the student clear his or her mind and revitalize a little bit before sitting for another hour or more.

- **Have a snack.** Students have hectic schedules that can make meals sporadic during the day. Taking time between classes to have a healthy snack can help eliminate the draw to junk food as well as the tiredness and inability to concentrate that might accompany hunger.

- **Run a quick errand.** Instead of making a separate trip later, students can use the time between classes to run quick errands such as stopping in the student union to pick up stamps or swinging by the library to return books.

- **Organize.** Students who arrive early can use the time to go through their book bags and get rid of all the junk that tends to accumulate.

SURVIVE THOSE CRAZY WEEKS

Successful students who create a schedule and stick to it do not suffer as much during the "crazy weeks" – the weeks with multiple exams, assignments, and projects due – as those who do not manage their time. This is mainly because students who manage their time have kept up with their classes all along, so there is not as much cramming to get it all done at the last minute. However, even the most organized students will feel the time crunch once in a while. Here are tips to help manage these weeks:

- **Stay healthy.** It is more important than ever during these weeks for students to continue exercising and eating right so their bodies can function with the added stress of later nights and more work.

🐚 **Take breaks.** It may seem there is no time for a break with so much to do, but successful students have found that when they are daydreaming or not getting far in their work, it is time to take a break – even if it is for only ten minutes.

🐚 **Work ahead.** Having a schedule that clearly illustrates everything is due on a certain week helps students set priorities and even get some things done early. There is no reason a project or paper cannot be done the week before it is due to leave time for studying for exams during the busy week.

CREATE A CLASS SCHEDULE

1. Determine how you spend your time now and figure out what things are most important to you. List five activities other than studying and classes (for example, things you do not want to give up for studying).

2. Determine which times of the day are best for you to study. Survey each of the following times of the day to help you determine which times are best for studying for you. Students who have schedules that vary widely from day to day may want to fill out this survey for each day. Another option would be to group days into similar schedules and complete the survey for each group of days.

   - Early morning
   - Midmorning
   - Midday (around lunchtime)
   - Afternoon
   - Late afternoon (about 3 until dinner)0-p-
   - Evening (after dinner until about 9)
   - Night

Energy Levels: Some people have high energy in the morning and others do at night. This is important to figure out because leisure activities should be completed during those times of low energy and studying should be completed during times of higher energy.

CREATE A CLASS SCHEDULE

Concentration Levels: This may vary from day to day. For example, if a student has a particularly mentally taxing class on Monday and Wednesday afternoons he will likely have a low concentration level in the late afternoon on those days. Other days, late afternoon may be a good time for him to study.

Friends' Activities: While this should not always be the determining factor on how you create your study schedule, it should have some impact. For example, if your friends spend every Thursday evening doing something together such as dinner and a movie it can be difficult to commit to a weekly study session at this time.

3. Graph out a weekly schedule, making sure the time blocks follow your university's schedule and add in all of your commitments including leisure activities and study blocks. Some students like to use a color coded schedule to help them see at a glance what type of activity they have scheduled.

Here is a schedule for a 14-credit load: Notice the number of hours spent studying. In this instance, Biology is a 5-hour-a-week class, but it does not require 15 hours a week of studying because the labs are largely in-class projects that do not require the 3:1 ratio of studying. Instead, this student decided to schedule a 1:1 studying ratio for the biology lab and lab review.

Mon	Tues	Wed	Thurs	Fri	Sat	Sun
Before 8 am						
wake up/ get ready	7am yoga	wake up/ get ready	7am yoga	wake up/ get ready	7am yoga	Sleep in/Free Time
8-9am	8-9:30am	8-9am	8-9:30am	8-9am	8-9am	
Biology Lecture	*Biology Lab*	*Biology Lecture*	*Biology Lab*	*Biology Review*		
9:10-10:10	9:40-11:10	9:10-10:10	9:40-11:10	9:10-10:10am	9-10am	
Workout/ Shower	*Freshman Comp*	Workout/ Shower	*Freshman Comp*	Workout/ Shower	*Study*	
10:20-11:20		10:20-11:20		10:20-11:20	10am-11am	
Study		*Study*		*Study*	*Study*	

Mon	Tues	Wed	Thurs	Fri	Sat	Sun
11:30-12:30	11:30-1pm	11:30-12:30	11:30-1pm	11:30-12:30	12-1pm	<u>Sleep in/Free</u>
Study	*Study*	*Study*	*Study*	*Study*	*Study*	
12:40-1:40pm	1:20-2:50pm	12:40-1:40pm	1:20-2:50pm	12:40-1:40pm	1-2pm	
Spanish I	*History 101*	*Spanish I*	*History 101*	*Spanish I*	*Study*	
1:50-2:50pm		1:50-2:50pm		1:50-2:50pm	2-3pm	
Study		*Study*		*Study*	*Study*	
3-5pm	3-5pm	3-5pm	3-5pm	3-5pm	3-5pm	
Study	*Study*	*Spanish Study Group*	*Study*	*Study*	*Study*	*Study*
5-7pm	5-6pm	5-6pm	5-6pm	5-6pm	5-6pm	5-6pm
<u>Dinner/ Hang Out w/ Friends</u>		*Study*	*Study*	*Study*	*Study*	*Study*
	6-7pm	6-7pm	6-7pm	6-7pm	6-7pm	6-7pm
	<u>Dinner/ Relax</u>	<u>Dinner/ Relax</u>	<u>Dinner/ Relax</u>	<u>Dinner/ Relax</u>	<u>Dinner/ Relax</u>	<u>Din/ Relax</u>
7:00-8:00pm						
After 8pm						

Key: *Italics* = Class, *Bold Italic* = Study Block, <u>Underlined</u> = Leisure Activities

CASE STUDY: AMBER WADE

Amber is a senior at the University of Wisconsin Oshkosh majoring in Secondary Spanish Education and working toward two minors: Bilingual Education and English as a Second Language. She is an intern at two elementary schools, works a part-time job and plans to graduate in December of 2008.

Amber's thoughts on the learning style:

The biggest surprise for me when it came to studying in college was that I actually had to study! In high school, I did not have to study. As long as I attended class, the quizzes and exams were easy enough to get a good grade. In college, quizzes and exams are far more difficult because professors tend ask specific questions and you have to answer, say, by writing an essay. In other words, you have to know your stuff! I remember, when I was in high school, I would joke around about how I would actually have to study in college and how it was going to be difficult. But I do not think I understood back then how true that was…it was not just something to joke around about.

Amber's thoughts on distractions and balancing time:

The number one thing that pulls me away from my studies is my computer/the Internet. It is so easy to "just take a quick break" and check my e-mail or see what is new on Facebook. Unfortunately, those "quick breaks" are far from being quick. Some other things that tend to pull me away from my studies are phone calls and remembering other things I need to do. It is helpful to make lists and turn off the computer and phone.

Amber's thoughts on mistakes:

One thing I regret is not using the resources on campus sooner, such as the Writing Center, tutors, sessions on how to study better, upperclassmen, professors, and the library for peace and quiet.

Amber's thoughts on hindsights:

One thing I wish I would have known about studying in college before I started college is that you cannot do it all! I am an organized, follow-the-rules, do-

CASE STUDY: AMBER WADE

well-in-school type person. In high school, I read every page of every book that my teachers told me to read, I completed every assignment thoroughly, and I did well on exams. When I got to college, it was overwhelming. In my opinion, professors ask you to accomplish more than you can actually get done in one semester if you are taking a full load of credits. In the beginning, I had a hard time coping with this. I felt as though I was failing and I was not being a good student because I was no longer reading every page of every book because I just did not have the time. Finally, I realized that it's okay! The important thing is to try your best and get as much accomplished as you POSSIBLY can. It is okay if you only proofread your paper three times instead of the four that your professor recommended.

Amber's thoughts on figuring out study tricks:

Creating to-do lists ahead of time helps me figure out what I need to get accomplished in a certain order, depending on due dates and how long an assignment will take to complete. Study or homework "appointments" make study time official. If I tell myself, "I have to work on Sunday and when I get home from work, I will write that paper," then I am more likely to do it.

Amber's thoughts on challenges:

I think the biggest challenge for college students when it comes to maintaining good grades is keeping that healthy balance between school and social life. Students get to college and have all of this freedom and they do not know how to handle that. Every opportunity they have to go to the bars, they will take it . . . they do not know how to say "no" because they have not experienced this freedom before. It is so important to realize that you must say "no" sometimes and other times, after you have your work done and you truly do have time to spare, you can reward yourself by going out.

Amber's thoughts on obstacles:

The biggest obstacle when it comes to studying for me is getting started. As a 5th year senior, I have learned over the years how to complete my work in little time, often the night before it is due. I do not necessarily consider this a good thing because I procrastinate since I am able to get my work done at the last minute. I know I would produce better quality work if I had started earlier.

FIND A STUDY SPOT

The best advice successful students give when it comes to finding the best study spots is: the more isolated, the better. College students may have difficulty with procrastination. The best defense against it is to eliminate the distractions. Additionally, fewer distractions allow for greater concentration.

HAVE MULTIPLE SPOTS

There is nothing worse than having to study for a huge exam and arriving at the sacred study spot only to find out that someone else got there first. Instances like this can throw off the entire mood and ruin a study session, especially when the student has to spend time searching for another good spot.

Here are some other reasons why successful students have more than one study spot:

- **Successful students** have several study spots around campus – preferably close to where they attend class – so they can pop into the closest one no matter where they are and not have to trek across campus every time they want to study.

- **Successful students** know when they need a change of scenery. When this happens, they pack up their things and head to the next closest spot to try again.

- **Successful students** realize they are not the only ones who know of these good spots and areas so even if their specific spot is open, there may be other people around who can be distracting.

KNOW WHICH SPOTS TO AVOID

Roommates and dorm mates are good, but they can be distracting. Dorms and apartments also provide the distractions of television, computer, and anything else that could be done except for studying. It is not unusual for students who are looking for ways to procrastinate to suddenly have the urge to clean, wash dishes, organize a desk, or anything but the task at hand. For these reasons, successful students know that serious studying must be done elsewhere, away from these distractions. They also know that dorms and apartments are not the only areas that make poor study spots:

- They are all over campus – large open areas full of tables and desks. They look like a perfect place to study and socialize and have a good time. This is partially true. These areas are nice for socializing and meeting with groups, but they are not nice for studying – serious studying, anyway. There are so many distractions that successful college students avoid these areas when they need to get something done.

- A study spot in close proximity to a good friend's study spot is also a recipe for disaster. Even the most successful student will say that studying close to a friend can result in a shortened study session because of the lure of visiting and eventually leaving the area to do something fun.

Some spots are too secluded. Students who tend to let their imaginations go wild should not go to an area completely secluded from other people. Before they know it, they will be thinking about all the things that could happen instead of concentrating on their studies.

KNOW WHERE TO LOOK

Finding good secret study spots requires some searching. Be on the lookout for a good place to go. One place to start is in the library, but not in the main study areas. Instead, look for tables and desks tucked away among the shelves. Students may also find good study areas in small department lounges that students may not know exist – they can be found by asking the professors if there is a student lounge or study room nearby.

Successful students choose study spots similar to where they will be using the information they are studying, such as a classroom. They should choose desks or tables with chairs over couches and other lounging furniture. This is because they have discovered that getting too relaxed while studying diminishes their ability to concentrate and retain information. There are other clues that a study spot may not be as good as it first appears:

Chilly or too warm rooms will not be comfortable for a long study session.

Rooms that open easily to high traffic areas may not be good because they can be prone to noise and the invitation of friends and acquaintances to stop in and chat.

Randomly open rooms or rooms open for short periods of time are not a good choice.

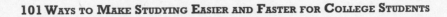

> Rooms with plenty of windows can cause the student to become easily distracted.

Keep a Secret

This is the hardest part, but it is important – successful students do not tell people about these prime study spots. A few things can happen by spreading the word. First, other people may want to try out the spots and they will become popular. Second, friends will start seeking the student out in these spots, causing the spot to lose the ability to be free of distractions.

FIND AND EVALUATE POTENTIAL SECRET STUDY SPOTS

Take a few hours and seek out a few good study spots. Start in the library by going away from the community study areas and looking in the stacks and other seemingly secluded areas. Then move to the classroom buildings and look for lounges and other study rooms that may be unknown to students.

Choose potential secret study spots and evaluate them using the following checklist. Write down notes to help you remember important information about the spot such as when it is open (or closed) to the public or notes about the conditions such as "it is a chilly room so bring a sweatshirt" or "noisy in the mornings when students are in the building."

- The spot is quiet.

- The spot is close to classes/dorm/apartment.

- The spot is in a building regularly open to students.

- The spot is rarely occupied by other students.

- The spot is secluded.

- The spot is comfortable.

- The spot has plenty of space for spreading out work.

- The spot has outlets for a computer or other necessary electronic devices.

PLAN WHERE YOU WILL STUDY AT EACH STUDY SESSION

Go back to your schedule and plan where you will study during each study session. It is best to note a back up location just in case the preferred location will not work for some reason. Here is an example with an excerpt from the previous schedule examples:

STUDY SCHEDULE					
8-9am	8-9:30am	8-9am	8-9:30am	8-9am	8-9am
Biology Lecture	Biology Lab	Biology Lecture	Biology Lab	Biology Lab Review	
9:10-10:10	9:40-11:10	9:10-10:10	9:40-11:10	9:10-10:10	9-10am
Workout/ Shower	Freshman Comp	Workout/ Shower	Freshman Comp	Workout/ Shower	Study Library, 3rd Floor
10:20-11:20		10:20-11:20		10:20-11:20	10-11am
Study Student Lounge		Study Student Lounge		Study Student Lounge	Study Library, 3rd Floor
11:30-12:30	11:30-1pm	11:30-12:30	11:30-1pm	11:30-12:30	9-10am
Study Student Lounge in For. Lang. Bldg	Study Library, 3rd Floor	Study Student Lounge in For. Lang. Bldg	Study Library, 3rd Floor	Study Student Lounge in For. Lang. Bldg	Study Library, 3rd Floor
12:40-1:40		12:40-1:40		12:40-1:40	1-2pm
Spanish I		Spanish I		Spanish I	Study Library, 3rd Floor

Dress for Success

It is tempting for students to dress in sweats and other comfortable clothes when they are getting ready for a long study session, but successful students have found that this is not best. When students wear sweats and other comfortable lounging clothes, they feel less like studying and more like partaking in leisure activities. This does not mean that successful students wear business attire or other formal clothing to class and to study, but they should get up and get ready for the day by presenting themselves in a manner that shows they mean business when it comes to classes and studying. Students agree that if they feel good about themselves they do better when it comes to school, work, and studies.

Appearance Does Matter

- Students who dress for class make a better impression on their professors.

- Students who get up, get dressed, and get going tend to be more energetic and willing to get to work even during "down" time.

- Students who dress for class make a better impression on their classmates and will be taken more seriously in study groups and other group activities.

- Students who show that they care about their appearance and strive to make a good impression on others will soon find that other people will have higher expectations of them. Students who have higher expectations set on them will strive to meet or beat these expectations. Likewise, lower expectations are set onto people who do not show that they care about their appearances.

GET ORGANIZED

The best time management, the perfect study spot, and the best study skills in the world cannot help the college student who is unorganized. Disorganization causes wasted time spent looking for supplies, paper, and other materials, and it also leads to a lack of focus. Successful students create a system that helps them keep everything together and easily accessible.

ORGANIZE THE BACKPACK

Backpacks can accumulate plenty of junk, but successful students know it is important to keep the junk to a minimum. Successful students also know to keep a few key items in the backpack, including extra paper, appropriate media supplies (such as flash drives), pens and pencils, spending money, and a few emergency snacks. This, in addition to the textbooks and notebooks for each class, should be enough to sustain the successful student for the day's worth of classes and study sessions.

Successful students have their own quirks when it comes to studying. Some like to listen to classical or other types of music to drown out outside noise, while others like to handle a stress ball. Some successful students have one

CD that they listen to only when studying and say that it helps them drown out outside distractions and get down to business. Whatever the quirk, successful students keep the necessary supplies in their backpacks at all times.

In addition to these items, successful students also know it is important to keep a stash of handy supplies in their bags "just in case." These include:

- A mini stapler

- A calculator

- Sticky notes – preferably a few different colors

- Notepads and notebooks

- Pens and highlighters in several different colors each

- A water bottle

- Ear plugs – for those times when it is impossible to find a quiet place to study

ORGANIZE THE PAPERS

Each student needs to find an individual method for organizing class materials for easy access. Some students like to have a large binder in which they keep all the syllabi, notes, and other materials for every class a master schedule for the semester. These students take notes on loose leaf paper while in class and then pop them into the binder in the proper section at the end of class. This also allows the students to put handouts and other materials from class right before or after the notes relating to them. Another benefit of using this type of organization is that students can combine or align class and lecture notes with notes taken from the text more easily than if they were taking notes in a spiral bound notebook. This is a good method for some students because it keeps everything together.

Not everyone likes this method because it can be bulky, and they do not like carrying all of the class information with them if they do not need it, or they prefer notebooks to loose leaf paper because it is less likely that the paper will get lost or disorganized. Here are some other options:

- Successful students who like the binder idea but do not like having all of their class materials in one large and heavy binder tend to like using one smaller binder for each class. This way they can keep all the information for each class organized and only need to carry the binders for the classes they will be working on that day.

- Other successful students benefit from color-coding everything. This means that all binders, notebooks, and folders for each class are a different color. Some even go as far as using color-coded sticky notes and media components, such as flash drives and disks.

- In the binders and folders, some students like to organize their materials by date while others prefer organizing it by topic.

ORGANIZE CLASS MATERIALS

Take out a sheet of paper and write down how you currently organize your class materials and answer the questions:

- Do you ever find yourself searching for class materials because you do not know where they are? If so, you need to rethink how you organize your information.

- Do you forget class materials that you need for a specific study session? If so, you need to plan your day the night before so you have everything you need with you.

- Do you like to carry all of your class materials with you all the time? If so, a binder method may work well for you.

- Do you like to be able to organize your material by topic? If so, you may want to look into using loose-leaf paper instead of notebooks.

- Do you ever grab the wrong folder or notebook for a certain class? If so, you may want to color code your class materials for easy recognition.

EVALUATE APPEARANCE AND ITS EFFECTS

Try it for a week. Get up every day and take the time to shower, get dressed in something other than pajama bottoms or sweats, and see the a difference it makes. Each night spend a few minutes evaluating your energy level, concentration and mood.

DETERMINE LEARNING STYLES & USE THIS KNOWLEDGE

Successful students know their preferred learning styles and how to use these styles to their advantage. There are different learning styles and various theories to go along with them.

ACTIVATE THE ACTIVE LEARNER

According to Richard M. Felder and Barbara A. Soloman in their article "Learning Styles and Strategies," active learners are those who need to use the information at hand to internalize, remember, and understand it. They prefer to do this through discussions and practical applications. Active learners tend to struggle in classes that consist primarily of lecture because they do not have the opportunity to discuss or use the information to internalize and understand it. According to Felder and Soloman, to be successful in these types of classes, students need to take the extra initiative to make up for this lack of active learning by doing it on their own. Suggestions for this include the following:

- Organizing a study group

- Spending time explaining the concepts to others

- Simulating problem solving in the area being discussed

- Asking the professor for ideas of activities that can help them actively process the information

- Seeking out interactive computer programs and CD-ROMs that can help them put the information to practical use

- Attending tutoring sessions that allow for groups to actively discuss the topics with the professor or a teacher's aide

ACTIVATE THE REFLECTIVE LEARNER

Reflective learners are those who prefer to think about the information before trying to talk about it or put it to use, and they prefer individual learning time. Reflective learners struggle when they are in fast-paced classes that do not allow time for thinking about the information. This could be a lecture, a discussion, or a lab that takes the entire class period. As Felder and Soloman point out, reflective learners can do things to give them the needed time to think about the information:

- Contemplate the assigned readings before class so they have a basis and ideas about what will be discussed.

- Review the reading assignment several times before class.

- Think about the material before and after class, figure out practical applications, and individually simulate problems and solutions related to the topic.

🐌 Immediately after class, spend time comparing the notes taken in class with those taken from the text and drawing connections and creating summaries.

🐌 Take time after class to digest the information. Students find this helpful if they look over the notes and add in thoughts and other ideas as they are reflecting.

BALANCE ACTIVE AND REFLECTIVE LEARNING

Felder and Soloman report that most students are active learners at some times and reflective learners at others. Students do tend to have a strong, moderate, or mild affinity toward one or the other; however, the best recommendation is for a solid balance between the two. Too much active learning can lead to problems part way into a project or study session and too much reflective learning can lead to the student spending too much time thinking and not enough time "doing. There are ways to achieve a balance:

🐌 Active learners can study with reflective learners as long as they are both open to listening to and using the other's perspective.

🐌 Active learners can make themselves slow down and think about the topic before jumping right in and doing whatever needs to be done.

🐌 Reflective learners can set a time limit for thinking about the topic before they begin their work.

ACTIVATE THE SENSING LEARNER

Felder and Soloman describe sensing learners as those who prefer learning facts and solving problems using tried-and-true methods. Sensing learners also like to memorize and to complete lab-type work that has a specific procedure. Over all, sensing learners are practical and need to see how the class applies to the real world. Sensing learners tend to struggle in classes that do not have a clear connection to the real world and to practical uses.

Sensing learners need to take the extra step to figure out how these concepts apply to the real world. They should:

- Ask the professor for clarifications.

- Attend a class discussion group where the members brainstorm real-world connections to help them internalize the information.

- Spend time making real-world connections on their own.

- Seek out additional sources that may have more information on how the topic applies to the real world.

- Use the examples in the text as a jumping board to create individual examples.

ACTIVATE THE INTUITIVE LEARNER

According to Felder and Soloman, intuitive learners do best by learning through discovery; they also tend to dislike repetition. Intuitive learners are quick to understand new concepts and are innovative in their studies. Intuitive learners dislike courses that require them to memorize and participate in repetitive work.

Intuitive learners are fairly lucky in college because the majority of classes require this type of thinking and application of concepts. Professors require innovative application of the information being studied instead of memorization and repetition of facts. There are exceptions to this rule, however, where intuitive learners find themselves in classes that require a large amount of memorization and repetitive work. Intuitive learners may become bored and find themselves making careless mistakes on exams and assignments because they do not like the repetitiveness of the questions They can take steps to help prevent problems in classes that tend to bore them, including the following:

- Make a concerted effort to pay special attention to the details, especially when completing exams and assignments.

- Ask around for recommendations of professors who do not conduct their classes in this manner before scheduling classes. There will be some subjects when this is unavoidable, however, due to the nature of the subject matter.

- Spend extra time studying by thinking about different ways the information can be used so that when the students have to complete the repetitive work, at least they have an idea of the type of purpose it serves.

ACTIVATE THE VISUAL LEARNER

Felder and Soloman define visual learners as those who need to see something to help them understand the material – such as pictures, timelines, demonstrations, films, and flow charts. Visual learners are also those who need to see how a word looks when they try to spell it.

Visual learners struggle in predominantly verbal classes. They can take extra steps to alleviate some of the stress, however, including the following:

- Seek out supporting materials for the text that often include CD-ROMs or links to Web sites that contain more information. Some textbooks also have companion books available that contain maps, graphs, pictures, and other graphics to go along with the information in the textbook.

- Take notes in the form of concept maps, graphs, charts, and timelines instead of outlines or lists.

- Use colored pens and highlighters to color code notes and make them more visually appealing.

- Create charts and other graphics from notes of the reading in anticipation of what the lecture will be about to help better visualize the information.

- Keep the textbook handy during the lecture so its graphics can be referred to while the professor is discussing the topic.

ACTIVATE THE VERBAL LEARNER

Verbal learners can be identified as those who can easily express themselves in the written or spoken context because they better understand information based on what they get out of written and spoken words. Verbal learners should take notes and write down key concepts and ideas in their own words. Verbal learners can also benefit from the following:

- Participating in study groups that discuss and explain the topics

- Reading, writing, and playing word games

- Using mnemonics to remember facts

- Creating rhymes and rhythms to remember facts and concepts

- Writing and rewriting notes

- Reciting information

While individual students may prefer either visual or verbal (visual learning may take precedence over verbal learning, according to Felder and Soloman), it is likely that most students learn best with a mixture of the two. This is a challenge for college students, however, because the vast majority of college levels classes rely on little visual information during class discussions and lectures.

ACTIVATE THE SEQUENTIAL LEARNER

Felder and Soloman describe sequential learners as those who like to figure out concepts in a logical, step-by-step fashion. Sequential learners can find solutions by following a set of formulas — even if they do not understand the information. The sequential learner can also be called the logical learner. These types of students tend to lean toward subjects like math. They also rely on lists, which can be useful when studying for an exam. Sequential learners have a difficult time in classes where the professor jumps around or does not explain all the steps. Sequential learners need to ask the professor to fill in the missing information or else seek out the information to fill it in on their own outside class. Other steps they can take to improve their learning include:

- Spend time after each class reorganizing notes into logical and sequential lists

- Join a study group to discuss the missing areas of information and to clarify facts

- Refer to the textbook to help them visualize the steps in the process being discussed

- Find additional resources to help them fill in the blanks in their notes by asking the professor or looking for reference material in the library or online

ACTIVATE THE GLOBAL LEARNER

Global learners are more random in their learning because they tend to work with large chunks of information and eventually just "get it." Global learners have a difficult time explaining how something works after they figure it out or how they got to the solution when they get there.

Global learners need to be able to see the big picture before they can internalize the information. They can feed their learning style by taking steps to see the big picture before delving too deeply into the details. This includes the following steps:

- Skimming a chapter before reading it so they can anticipate what is coming up next

- Paying attention to the syllabus so they can see how each class's topics relate to the next

- Writing down the thought processes that led up to them figuring out how something works so they can replicate it in the future

- Pairing up with sequential learners who may be able to help them see how all the details contribute to the solution instead of just looking at the big picture

ACTIVATE THE AURAL LEARNER

Aural learners are those who learn best with sound. This can mean rhyming, music, or listening to the content. Aural learners can benefit by reading their notes into a tape recorder and then listening to them. Aural learners also benefit from using mnemonics and jingles to help them learn – such as changing the words to a popular song to fit the information being studied. They can use their preferred learning style to their advantage by using the following techniques:

- Choosing lecture-based classes whenever possible

- Studying in areas that allow them to recite notes and listen to recordings of notes

- Participating in discussion groups

- Looking for auditory supplements to the text, such as sound recordings

ACTIVATE THE PHYSICAL LEARNER

The physical learner is the one who needs to work with his or her hands to internalize the information. Physical learners need demonstrations and the ability to participate in the process. Even when physical objects are not available for manipulations, physical learners should try the following suggestions:

- Rely on writing and drawing – one way to do this is to use large paper and make big drawings and words.

- Act out the process or concepts, such as role playing events in history.

- Ask the professor for help in finding manipulators related to the topic.

- Create models and dioramas that depict the topic.

CHOOSE THE RIGHT TEXTBOOK AND MATERIALS

The professor chooses the textbook for the class, but successful students take advantage of some of the choices they have in the textbook. Textbook publishers offer CD-ROMs and other supporting material — in the form of graphs, diagrams, maps, and other visuals. These items are included in new books or can be purchased separately. Furthermore, an increasing number of publishers are now offering an Internet code with the purchase of new books to allow the student to access supporting materials online. Students who have questions about this should speak to a university bookstore representative or to their professors to get more information about the materials available.

Students who accept and embrace their learning styles by following the recommendations for their preferences will soon see they can use their study time more efficiently. They will enjoy studying more if they choose activities that agree with their preferences instead of fighting the way their minds are inclined to learn. Before long, this enjoyment of studying will increase their enjoyment in the subject matter, even if it is a class they did not choose to take.

IDENTIFY LEARNING STYLES

Use the quick guide beginning below to help you determine which learning styles you lean towards. Read through the characteristics in each section and highlight the section(s) that best describe your studying and learning tendencies. After you have completed this, use the key at the bottom of the table to identify your learning styles.

LEARNING STYLE A	LEARNING STYLE B
Prefer classes that involve memorization of facts and other information.	Learn better with visual depictions of the information such as a timeline, chart, graph, or demonstration.
Need to know how the information/topics/concepts apply to the practical world to be able to understand its importance.	Struggle in classes where much of the information is provided through lecture with minimal use of visual aids.

LEARNING STYLE C	LEARNING STYLE D
Can see the whole picture but the details are fuzzy. Know the answer or solution to a problem but cannot explain the steps to reach that solution. Need to be able to see the big picture before even thinking about how the details fit together.	Prefer classes that require or allow hands-on applications of the material. Like to see demonstrations and prefer to be able to participate in the process. Do well when they use physical objects or manipulators to help learn a concept. Use role playing to act out scenes to help internalize information.
LEARNING STYLE E	**LEARNING STYLE F**
Can easily express ideas through writing and speaking. Prefer lectures over demonstrations and labs. Enjoy working with study groups that focus on discussing the information.	Like to use music, rhyming, or other rhythmic methods to help remember information. Enjoy lecture-based classes. Benefit from taping notes and listening to them repeatedly.
LEARNING STYLE G	**LEARNING STYLE H**
Use the information to understand it. Like to discuss the information with teachers and classmates. Prefer labs, practical application, and discussions over lectures.	Prefer to use formulas to find answers and understand concepts. Use lists and other step-by-step formulas for studying and understanding the material.
LEARNING STYLE I	**LEARNING STYLE J**
Need time to think about information before discussing or applying it. Prefer studying alone over studying with a group. Dislike participating in class discussions if there has not been time to digest the information first.	Dislike classes that require memorization of facts and other information. Become bored with classes that require the repetitive use of concepts and formulas. Prefer to learn through discovery instead of being told all the information up front.

Key:
A = Sensing, B = Visual, C = Global, D = Physical, E = Verbal, F = Aural, G = Active,
H = Sequential, I = Reflective, J = Intuitive.

EVALUATE LEARNING METHODS

In the following table, list your current classes at the top of the blank columns.
In the rows, list your preferred learning styles. Then, in each space, list two or
three specific things you can do to use your learning style preference to help
you succeed in your class.

	GENERAL TIPS	CLASS #1	CLASS #2	CLASS #3	CLASS #4
CLASS					
LEARNING STYLE #1					
LEARNING STYLE #2					
LEARNING STYLE #3					
LEARNING STYLE #4					

CASE STUDY: JAMES FRANKLIN HICKS, III

James Franklin Hicks, III is a student at the
University of South Carolina Upstate majoring in
Speech Communication and minoring in Political
Science.

James' thoughts on the learning style:

The hardest thing about studying in college is balancing the priorities of which
class to study the most. You may have situation where you have two classes that
demand most of your studying time and then you have maybe one to three classes
that demand a little less studying than the other two.

CASE STUDY: JAMES FRANKLIN HICKS, III

The biggest surprise was that studying for college was different than studying for high school. The subject matter was more concentrated than in high school.

James' thoughts on mistakes:

The biggest mistakes I've made were underestimating the amount of studying needed for particular classes. I recognize the mistake after the first test, exam, or quiz. There may be plenty of time to correct the problem.

James' thoughts on hindsight:

One thing that I wish I would have known about studying in college is that just about every class has a different structure. You have to adapt your studying style to every class.

James' thoughts on figuring out study tricks:

One of the best tricks I have found that helps me study or prepare for a class is attending all the lectures.

James' thoughts on challenges:

Maintaining good grades requires prioritizing your classes. If someone can identify early on which classes they are going to have a hard time in versus those they may have an easier time in it is a crucial step in getting a head start on earning good grades.

James' thoughts on obstacles:

Balancing the extra-curricular activities is possible the biggest obstacle in studying. The best way to overcome it is to make sure the priorities in your college life are in order. Don't go to that organizational meeting when you have to study for a class.

Part 2

GETTING DOWN TO BUSINESS:

WHAT TO DO EVERY DAY

Studying is more than hitting the books the night before a quiz or exam or quickly throwing together a project. Successful students know that if they do a little bit each day they will be able to take exams and complete assignments and projects with much less stress than if they put things off until they "need" it. Keeping up with the little things makes the big things easier when the time comes.

READING FOR COMPREHENSION: GENERAL READING TIPS

College classes require substantial reading that can be overwhelming and seemingly impossible to keep up with. Furthermore, many students may feel like it is a huge waste of time because they read and promptly forget what they have read. The problem with this is the reading material is required for tests, but it may not have been discussed in class. The following tips will help students improve their reading comprehension.

READ OFTEN

Successful students spend much of their time reading. This helps build a wealth of background information that can help them understand, relate to, and even apply new knowledge when reading for a class. This reading can be leisurely and it can be fiction or non-fiction. It can be a book, a newspaper, or even web pages on the Internet. As long as it is building the student's knowledge base, it will be beneficial. Students who spend much of their time reading may display the following characteristics:

- They tend to know about current events.

- They can relate subject matter to other topics.

- They have a broader base from which to build new knowledge.

- They seem able to read more efficiently than their counterparts who do not do much leisurely reading.

- They have a hobby they can do virtually anywhere – even between classes, when they need a break from studying.

- They build their vocabulary, which will help them when reading for class.

SET A PACE

Successful students have figured out there is a certain pace that can help them get through their reading assignments as quickly as possible without compromising comprehension of the material. This pace differs for everyone. Students should re-evalute this reading pace often.

Successful students know that a reading pace needs to be flexible. Depending on the material, it may be a faster or slower read than the previous assignment. Also, the time of day and level of distractions can affect reading speed. This is why it is important to continually evaluate the success of the reading and to adjust whenever necessary. The reading pace may be too fast if the students are having these problems:

- Rereading large portions of text

- Not finding any main points in large portions of the text

- Promptly forgetting what they read

🕮 Not fully understanding the concept being discussed

🕮 Being unsure which information to mark for further review

The reading pace may be too slow if the student is having these problems:

🕮 Consistently writing more notes than will fit into the margin

🕮 Inability to keep the flow of the text going or difficulty connecting information from one section to another because there is too much time in between

🕮 Becoming bored with the content

PREPARE BEFORE READING

One of the best ways to get the most out of a reading assignment is to establish a basis of types of information the assigned reading will contain. This can be done in several ways. Successful students use the following techniques:

🕮 **Looking over the book to get a sense of the layout.** Successful students review the book noting the types of external material found in sidebars, charts, graphs, and margins

🕮 **Evaluating the length of the chapters.** Successful students do not get bogged down and bored with a topic because they follow the rule of ten, meaning they do not read more than ten pages of a chapter in one sitting. Breaking down chapters makes reading the material easier because a ten-page chapter sounds better than a forty- or fifty-page chapter.

🕮 **Skimming through several pages** to see what the reading will be like.

Reading the introduction, conclusion, and summaries.

Looking for a pattern of typographical cues. Bolded, italicized, underlined, or bulleted lists are the words and ideas the author wants to emphasize. Knowing how the author uses these cues will help the student anticipate what to look for. Successful students know they need to figure out why these items are highlighted and fit them into the bigger picture of the meaning of the text.

Thinking about what you are going to read before you read it. Students look through the textbook and read the headings and subheadings. While doing this, they think about what they already know about the subject. This helps them anticipate what they will be reading; it also helps them generate questions about what they would like to know.

This process does not have to be time-consuming. It can be done in as little as five minutes, and after a student has a feel for a book, the basis does not need to be re-established. The one exception to that, however, would be for students who want to do a "mini" preparation at the beginning of each chapter to give them an overview of what the chapter will contain.

Look for an Organizational Pattern

The reading assignment will have an organizational pattern of some sort. Students who get to know the organizational pattern before reading will have a better sense of what to expect. Possible types of organizational patterns include listing a sequence, following a process, progressing through a place, listing items by importance, comparing multiple items, or listing cause and effects.

Anticipating the organizational pattern can help students with the following tasks:

- Figuring out how they are going to organize their notes

- Anticipating when and where in the text their questions will be answered

- Systematically working their way through the text

- Picking out the most important topics

- Getting a sense for how the author will be approaching the information

Focus on the Ideas

Successful students know it can be difficult to see the whole picture, but when they focus on the ideas of the paragraph, page, or chapter, it is easier to recall the facts and details later. By focusing on the specific details while reading, some students fail to see the whole picture and main ideas. Successful students use different techniques to help them keep their focus on the ideas instead of the small details. These techniques include the following:

- Allowing themselves to only highlight one phrase or idea per paragraph

- Reading several paragraphs before writing anything down

- Asking and answering questions about the text

- Reviewing and revising notes that contain keywords while thinking or reciting the facts that go with them

- Using concept maps or other visual guides to connect the ideas to each another

Reading the conclusion to see how the author connects and applies the ideas in the reading

TAKE STEPS TO REDUCE ZONING

Even the most successful students can zone out while reading. It is easy to do and frustrating because they need to go back and reread what they have just read. Here are some tips that successful students use when they are reading:

- **Read with intonation** (reading it how it would be spoken). This does not mean reading aloud. It is possible to read silently and still read with intonation. It is useful because it requires the reader to spend more time looking at and understanding what is written and how it should sound rather than mindlessly scanning the words without paying attention to what they are saying. Reading with intonation also makes reading more memorable because it adds feeling and emotion to the text – it can even help the reader get a sense of the personality of the writer based on how the words sound and come together with intonation.

- **Take breaks.** Successful students know the importance of not forcing things. If reading a text is not working, it is a good time to take a break and switch to a different subject or assignment, at least for a while.

- **Stop and make a list.** Zoning while reading means students are thinking about other things instead of what they are reading. When this happens, successful students take a minute to make a to-do list about whatever it is that keeps creeping into their thoughts, whether it is what to pack for a weekend trip or what to get at the grocery store later that afternoon. Writing it down will help clear it from the mind.

Master the Art of Skimming

Skimming is one of the steps that successful students use to help them become acquainted with the textbook and reading assignment, there are times when skimming should take precedence over reading word for word:

- Skimming is appropriate when the student is searching for something specific.

- Skimming is a way to review, especially when the student is answering questions about the reading and needs to refresh his or her memory on what was in the section.

- Skimming can be beneficial if the student is already knowledgeable about the topic and wants to make sure no new information is provided.

- Skimming helps students clarify misunderstandings in the notes or discrepancies between notes taken from the text and notes taken during a lecture. It helps the student quickly find the area where the specific topic is being discussed.

Warning: Skimming is not a good idea for any students who are reading for comprehension.

Recognize Signal Words

Successful students look for "signal" words when reading to help them anticipate the main points. Walter Pauk illustrates these words in his book, *How to Study in College*. Here are some of the examples:

- Words that indicate examples are "specifically," "for example," "for instance," and "to illustrate." These words are clues that students should make sure they understand the concept before trying to decipher the example.

🕮 Words that indicate cause and effect are "consequently," "as a result," "accordingly," and "hence." These words are clues that the effect is about to be illustrated. It is important for students to verify they understand the cause.

🕮 Words that indicate enumeration – "first," "second," and "third" — tell students they need to make sure they understand all the steps in the process being illustrated.

🕮 Words that indicate contrast such as "on the other hand," "however," and "despite," tell students to make sure they understand both sides of the issue.

🕮 Words that indicate comparison are "likewise," "similarly," and "identical." These words tell students to be aware of all the similar things.

STEP BACK IN TIME

Successful students who are studying a difficult subject or concept or who are reading from a difficult book may want to look at lower-level materials for clarification of the topic. This concept works well for topics in the science and history fields. Successful students find this gives them enough background on the topic to go back and gain a more thorough understanding of the text.

Here are some books that can be used for background on topics:

🕮 Greenhaven Press Publishing offers a series of books titled Opposing Viewpoints. These cover a variety of social topics and each contains articles about various sides of the issues. They work to promote critical thinking about the topic at hand.

🕮 The We Were There series gives real-life accounts of people in history. Each book focuses on a different event, time period, or issue in history.

🕮 The Magic School Bus is a series of fictional books that explore a science theme or topic in each book. The children in the book board the magic school bus with their teacher and find themselves in predicaments that require the use of science knowledge to solve the problems and get back home.

USE THE LIBRARY'S REFERENCE MATERIALS

Successful students learn that relying solely on the textbook is not the best way to gain a thorough understanding of information. Students find the library's reference section is a place to gain their bearing before diving into a new topic. The reference section contains encyclopedias, dictionaries, and specialized reference books that give short and understandable definitions and explanations. For example, before reading an entire chapter on the functions of the brain, a student may want to consult an encyclopedia to get a basic sense of how the brain looks and where the different sections are located. Another example is consulting an atlas to get a sense of where the cities and towns are located in a specific country before reading a chapter on that country's history.

Here are some descriptions to help students determine which resources will help them:

🕮 Dictionaries are used for finding the definitions and usages of words. If successful students come across a word that seems to be important in the text but they cannot make sense of its use in this context, they can go to the dictionary to see if there are usages of the word of which they are unaware.

🕮 Atlases are appropriate for studying recent history, social studies, geography, and cultures. They help the students visualize where and why certain things happened.

🕮 Encyclopedias give slightly more detailed definitions of words than dictionaries do and they have the added benefit of including people, places, and events that may not appear in the dictionary. While their explanations are more detailed than the dictionary, encyclopedias are more straightforward than textbook explanations.

🕮 Law books are good for looking up court cases and laws that may be referenced in other texts without a clear explanation.

🕮 Religion and mythology encyclopedias are good resources for deciphering references in fiction and non-fiction readings. Religion and mythology are frequently referred to in texts, and if students are unaware of the specific story or religion they may not be able to understand the concept.

🕮 Medical dictionaries can help students look up ailments, diseases, and questions about anatomy when they need clarification to help them understand a reading.

🕮 CD-ROMs and online databases contain a wealth of information. Colleges and universities have access to a variety of these resources to help the students. Students who are unsure of what is available should make an appointment with a librarian or media specialist.

APPLY THE MATERIAL

Successful students often do more than read and take notes on the texts. They take the time — not necessarily immediately after finishing the reading — to process the information and find ways to apply it to their lives. For example, if they just finished reading a math textbook that explained the theory behind a certain math function, they may spend time figuring out how this specific math function actually applies to their lives and how they may use it, other than to just pass the upcoming assignments and exams. Successful students can apply the material for specific curricular areas to their lives in the following examples:

History

- Putting themselves in the middle of a historic event. This includes examining feelings and anticipating actions. It can also include practicing problem solving to determine how and why people made the decisions they made.

- Thinking about what they would have liked or disliked about living in that time period.

English

- Putting themselves in the middle of a fictional work and examining how they would react in such a situation. Other ways to apply fictional work to their lives are to determine who they would be friends or enemies with and why, what advice they would give the characters, and what their reactions to situations would be versus the reactions of the characters in the book.

- Examining how they use grammar and other English topics on a regular basis and trying to implement one change at a time.

Foreign Languages

- Trying to add one or two new phrases from what they read into their daily vocabulary for a few days until they know what it means and how to use it.

- Comparing their own lives with the culture(s) they read about. This includes comparing, contrasting, and examining how they would feel living in the other culture.

Science

- Thinking about how the concepts relate to their daily lives. Thinking about how the studies and research related to the concept improve their lives.

- Developing hypotheses on how the concepts could be used to solve problems they face on a regular basis.

GENERAL READING SKILLS CHEAT SHEET	
Read Often	Expand knowledge, apply material, improve reading speed, portable hobby, and increase vocabulary
Set a Pace	Adjust when rereading, when not finding main points, when forgetting what has been read, and when not understanding concept
Prepare First	Understand layout to help predict what will be next, think about length of sections, and observe typographical cues
Look for Patterns	Understand the text organization to help organize notes, anticipate questions and answers, and find main points
Focus on Ideas	Avoid getting hung up on the details and try to look at the whole picture first
Skim	Help find specific information and prepare for a review
Signal Words	Recognize and understand the importance of words that signify important information
Simplify Information	Use lower-level texts to clarify a concept before delving into the more complicated details present in college-level texts

GENERAL READING SKILLS CHEAT SHEET	
Use Resources	Clarify misunderstandings and confusion with the library's resource section
Apply the Material	Think about how and why this information is important in real life

CASE STUDY: ALAN GREY, STUDENT

Alan Gray is a freshman at Florida Atlantic University's Wilkes Honors College in Jupiter. A candidate for his bachelors of arts degree in liberal arts and sciences, Alan plans on attending law school after graduating from college and intends to practice criminal law.

Alan's thoughts on the learning style:

The biggest surprise for me when it came to studying in college was how much more difficult studying in college is than it was in high school. I think this was because teachers guided you toward what you needed to study in high school, spoon-feeding you information about what specifically would be on the test and what you needed to study.

Alan's thoughts on distractions and balancing time:

The terrific thing about being in college is that it opens more social possibilities for you: parties, eating out, video game parties, watching movies or TV shows, just hanging out with friends, and so much more. Unfortunately, these opportunities are also distracting. I balance my time by designating times of the week when I need to study. During other times, I relax and hang with my friends, but I won't hesitate to cut that time short if there's more studying to be done.

Alan's thoughts on mistakes:

My biggest mistake in terms of college and studying was assuming that I could function the same way in college that I did in high school. For example, I was practically fluent in Spanish for most of high school, and did not need to do more than gloss over information that would appear on the test. I tried that on my first college Spanish test, though, and realized that would not work.

CASE STUDY: ALAN GREY, STUDENT

Alan's thoughts on hindsight:

The one thing I wish I had known about studying in college before I started was the value of friends in the same class. At the end of my first semester, I realized that studying and reviewing in groups was so much more effective than trying to accomplish the same by myself. Among my friends, we can bounce questions off each other, make sure we understand everything, and even have a few laughs. It's so much more time-consuming, difficult, and boring to study alone.

Alan's thoughts on figuring out study tricks:

Two words: flash cards. They are my savior! Writing them out is also helpful in the studying process, since I need to read and write each term and its definition. They are helpful in many classes, not just with word-definition type questions, but with theories, dates and events, and more.

Alan's thoughts on challenges:

The biggest challenge to maintaining good grades is to balance your school work with everything else that goes on in your collegiate life: extracurricular activities, social life, relationships, work, etc. If a college student can learn to effectively balance each of these things in their study routines, then he or she should have no trouble maintaining good grades.

Alan's thoughts on routines:

My study routine is to designate certain time slots throughout the course of the week where I only study. This, of course, changes depending on my course schedule each semester, but the practice is effective in blocking off time periods for work, and others to play.

Alan's thoughts on obstacles:

The biggest obstacle when it comes to studying is balancing it with your social life. I am tempted to simply abandon studying and hang out with my friends. To overcome it, I first try to get all my studying done in one of my designated study periods. If there is more that needs to be done, then I evaluate my need to study — Do I have enough time to take a break? Is this a paper, project, or assignment due tomorrow? On Monday? Next week? Next month? If I go out tonight, will I still be able to get my work done in a timely manner?

READ WITH A SYSTEM: SQ3R & BEYOND

During World War II, Francis P. Robinson designed the SQ3R system to help military personnel read and study faster. A proven and successful system, SQ3R had some drawbacks that led students to modify the steps to fit their needs better.

UNDERSTAND THE BASIC SQ3R SYSTEM

The basic SQ3R system asks students to take five steps when reading and understanding a text: Survey, Question, Read, Recite, and Review.

🕮 In the Survey step students preview the text and get a feel for how the information is organized. They read through the headings, subheadings, summaries, and conclusions. This step should be quick – students should be able to survey the text in a minute or two and get a sense of what ideas will be covered. It also helps the students mentally organize the material as they are reading it, because they know to expect.

🕮 In the Question step, students think about questions for each section and subsection of the book as they read it. For example, in this chapter of this book, students could ask themselves "What are the proven techniques?" and "How does the basic SQ3R system work?" The question step has two main purposes. First, it takes a conscious effort to formulate and think about the questions, which prevents mindless reading. Second, the student automatically starts thinking about the information they already know that can answer the question. It gives them a background to build on as they are reading.

🕮 In the Read step, students read the section and look for the answers to the questions they formulated for the section or subsection.

🕮 In the Recite step, students read the section and recite, in their own words, a summary of what they have read. Putting it into their own words requires the students to understand what they have read. Students who are unable to answer the questions for the section should go back to the read step and try again.

🕮 In the Review step, students go back through the chapter by reading the headings and mentally noting what information was under each heading. It gives the student a basic summary of the chapter and allows them to note whether there are any sections that they need to go back and work on some more.

The SQ3R system is a logical, step-by-step system that allows students to have a plan to help them actively read the material and ingrain it in their minds instead of mindlessly looking at the words and not getting much out of the material.

Try it Out

Here is a sample of what the SQ3R method might look like.

BOOK EXCERPT

(Excepted from *101 Businesses You Can Start With Less Than One Thousand Dollars: For Students* by Heather Shepard.)

Are You up for Self-employment?

Self-employment is not for everyone; you will have to decide if self-employment is the best thing for you. It is important to get feedback from your family and those closest to you. Allow them to address the concerns and thoughts they may have about your venture. Building a business takes dedication in the first year.

Considering your current role as a student, decide what you specifically think you would gain from starting your own business.

While starting your own business offers advantages, as a student there are some specific advantages to starting a business, including:

Financial Freedom – When you work for someone else you get paid only for the time you actually work. When you work for yourself, you make money 24 hours a day, 7 days a week, especially if you are selling on the Web.

Flexible Hours – When you work for yourself you have the advantage of creating a schedule that can bend or change as necessary so you can maintain your current school schedule. You can work more during breaks and take time off for exam week.

Your Time, Your Training – When you work for yourself, you decide what is important for you to know. You will earn hands-on training in a variety of subjects. In a corporate job you would be limited to one job and one set of duties and responsibilities.

Responsibility – As your own boss, you are responsible for the successes or disappointments you face. As it stands right now, if you are working for someone else, you are giving that person control over your situation. By taking control of your future, you have no one to blame but yourself for your difficulties. On the other hand, you have no one to praise but yourself when you create a successful and marketable business.

Experience – Owning your own business will give you the experience you need to succeed in any endeavor in the future, even if your business fails.

Survey: Students should notice that there will be five main points in this section and that the theme of the section is about determining if the reader is up for self-employment.

Questions:

- What are the qualities a person needs to be ready for self-employment?

- How does financial freedom relate to self-employment?

- How do flexible hours relate to self-employment?

- How does training relate to self-employment?

- How does responsibility relate to self-employment?

- How does experience relate to self-employment?

Read: Students would read through the section and think about the answers to each of the questions. Some students might highlight or underline the answers or they might write notes in the margins.

What are the qualities a person needs to be ready for self-employment?

A willingness for financial freedom, a desire to have flexible hours, the ability to train for and complete many different jobs, the responsibility to face the challenges, the desire to gain experience as a business owner.

How does financial freedom relate to self-employment?

Self-employment allows the business owner to earn money at whatever rate they wish, not just for the hours they put in at a regular job.

How do flexible hours relate to self-employment?

Self-employed students and make their work schedule fit around their school schedule.

How does training relate to self-employment?

Self-employed students can train for and work in any role they want in the business, not what is dictated by a boss.

How does responsibility relate to self-employment?

Self-employed students are responsible for the successes and failures of their businesses.

How does experience relate to self-employment?

Self-employed students can gain experience to help them in the future.

Recite: Students would then recite the answers to each of the questions.

Review: Students would read through the section by looking at the headings and saying in their own words what information is under each heading.

Build On the System

Successful students know they need to be flexible when it comes to using proven systems and are able to adapt them to meet their needs. For example, in the SQ3R system, a student may not like reciting the information aloud – or may be in a library where that is not possible – so they think about the answers, write them down, or type them on the computer. Students need to take the proven techniques and mix and match the methods to fit their needs so that they are successful for them.

For example, some students take the SQ3R method and build on it to find a method that works for them. Here are some other techniques that students have found successful when building on the SQ3R method:

- Successful students take the time to ask questions. They do this before starting to read – they think about the topic and list or think about what questions they would like answered on that topic.

- Successful students who are struggling with comprehension of the text or pulling together ideas of a section shift to questioning and summarizing after each paragraph. They then write their questions, answers, or summaries in the margins or a notebook for easy review later.

- Some successful students do not want to take the time to ask the obvious questions and prefer to summarize instead. These students may choose to make a longer summary at the end of each page or section instead of after the end of each paragraph. This is a useful technique for less difficult material and when concentration levels are still high enough to retain the information. Again, the summaries should be written in a notebook or the margin of the book for easy access later.

- Successful students often write the questions in the margins and underline or highlight the key words in the paragraph that answer the questions.

- Some successful students know that highlighting and underlining an entire paragraph is not useful when going back to review, so they focus on just the key words and phrases.

- Some successful students immediately try to apply the information by asking (and answering) how they can use it at the end of each section.

- Successful students do not overlook the "why" or "how" question. This happens when the original question is answered quickly in the paragraph and there is more information. For example, if a student reading this book asked, "Why do students build on the system?" they can find their answer quickly in the first paragraph. Asking "How" after that will help them recognize that the tips in this bulleted list give them important and useful information as well.

- Successful students take extra action when they do not feel they understand the text. They take time to figure out and detail anything what they do not understand. This extra effort helps them figure it out, but if it does not, they know what questions to ask when they seek help from outside sources.

- Successful students understand the importance of reflecting on what they have read and reviewed. Reflectors take the ideas a step further than memorizing them and internalize the information by thinking about it, applying it, and coming up with innovative solutions (even if hypothetical) to the problems. They jot down questions for further clarification from the professor or for things they need to go back into the reading to find.

- Successful students realize that one of the downfalls of the SQ3R method is it does not promote curiosity inside the text. Asking questions throughout the reading process promotes a proactive approach to learning, which indicates the student is thinking about and analyzing the information as he or she processes it and also indicates he or she is not simply reading to forget in a few minutes. If the student was reading about electrical circuitry and they came across a passage that stated parallel circuits are better for larger venues, the student may ask, "Why are they better?" Successful students take advantage of this curiosity and look for the answers to their natural questions as they are reading. If the student cannot find the answer in the text, it should be jotted down for further research.

EVALUATE THE RESULTS

After developing and using a system, students need to evaluate how it is working for them. They can do this by comparing how the lecture followed the information they studied and reviewed, how well they think they know the material a few days after studying, and how the test questions related to the questions they generated.

Students can also mentally review the information and jot down any further questions they have about the topic to go back to the book and clarify the answers or find more information from another source.

This is important for several reasons:

- Students who do not evaluate their reading methods may be missing the mark based on how the professor is using the material.

- Reading methods may need to be tweaked or altered for each class depending on the style of the textbook, how the professor handles the information in the text versus information in the lecture, and how the student feels about the subject matter of the class. Students who do not care for the material need to make an extra effort to actively read.

- No reading method is perfect all the time. There may be room for improvement and successful students know this, so they understand there will be situations when they need to change things.

READ WITH A PLAN: NOTE-TAKING STRATEGIES

Even with all of the previously mentioned reading tips, some students like specific methods of taking notes on what they have read so they can easily go back and review it whenever they want. Also, successful methods of note taking while reading can increase the active learning taking place throughout the reading process.

FORGET WHAT YOU HAVE BEEN TAUGHT

Up until college, it is taboo to write in books. As a college student, however, it is important to write in your books as needed. Any student who looks at a used textbook in the bookstore knows previous students have embraced this concept as well.

Useful ways to write in the book include the following:

- Underlining

- Circling

- Highlighting

- Taking notes

- Asking and answering questions

- Marking areas for further review

- Using stickers and sticky notes to mark important areas

Successful students have systems – from the incredibly simple to the painstakingly complicated – to help them when it comes to taking notes from a text.

Beware of Used Books

Used textbooks have a certain lure in the bookstore. They are considerably cheaper than the newer version, but this cheaper cost comes with a price:

- Markings from previous owners can be confusing and misleading – especially when a student assumes they can just skim the markings of the previous student. The biggest problem with doing this is there is no indication of whether these markings and notations were successful.

- Students have different methods to get the most out of the text. One person's method may not mesh with the next; the markings of the previous owner may get in the way of the markings of the current owner.

- Used books may not come with all the supplemental material that the new versions do. This may not be a problem for all students or for all textbooks, but active readers and note takers like to have as much material and as many resources as possible at their disposal.

When looking for textbooks in the book store, students who want to get the most out of their texts should buy new or at least find those with the least amount of markings and notations. It will cause fewer distractions when reading and studying the material.

LOVE THE BOOK

Successful students take caring for their books to an extreme. When they use their books to get the most out of them, they have to love them and make them their own. They can do this by using their system of notations, marking certain pages, and adding sheets of notes and questions in pages they want to explore more. Any student who has seen the books loved by professors has noticed the questions, markings, and added notes and can see the book has been referred back to numerous times.

Students who have mastered the art of notating texts come supplied with different colored pens and highlighters, sticky notes, and note paper. They have all the supplies to mark material for different reasons as well as take notes and slip them into the book where needed. Sticky notes are useful to mark important pages because they can stick out of the book without falling out.

Signs that successful students have properly loved their books:

- The spines are no longer stiff.

- The covers are worn.

- The pages are colorful.

- Fanning the book causes pages of handwritten notes to fall out.

- Sticky notes decorate the edges of the pages.

- Corners are folded and refolded to mark pages.

- Questions, answers, and comments fill the margins.

- Diagrams and sketches of graphs, charts, and concept maps appear in blank spaces.

READ FIRST, NOTATE LATER

It is easy for students to get carried away with marking. When a reader highlights an entire paragraph, it means they are not actively reading and thinking about what they have read.

It is important for students to read a paragraph or a section and then go back and highlight, question, mark, and think about the material. These are the processes that require notations in the text and the results of these processes will give the reader a better understanding of the text and enough information to spark his or her memory of what was read.

Students who notate to their advantage practice the following techniques:

- Stopping after every paragraph or section. They go back and question, comment on, and synthesize what they have read.

- Asking "why," "when," and "how" to determine what the main points of the text are.

- Only highlighting main points and phrases.

- Writing meaningful comments in the margins.

- Using the margins to indicate which areas need further research or explanations.

- Highlighting key words in the text. Some students use a different colored highlighter or pen to make key words stand out and then link it to the definition, explanation, and usages of the word in the text.

- Paying attention to the supplementary material in the text. After reading the paragraph or section, they go back and study the marginal comments, graphs, charts, inserts, and sidebars – whatever information the author included – and link it back to the text.

BE SPECIFIC AND SELECTIVE

Students who do not know how to actively read texts or have a system to help them internalize the material as they are reading mark or highlight sentences and phrases throughout the text. They may take the time to write a notation, such as "important," in the margin or put an exclamation point next to important details.

While these actions are useful in the right context, they are not specific. Instead of writing "important," successful students jot down why it is important: "three reasons why people forget" or "author's definition of 'community'." These specific notations in the margins should be paired with equally specific markings in the text. The first example should have highlighted the three reasons. The second example should have the key words and phrases of the definition highlighted in the text.

Avoid getting bogged down with too much information and highlighting and notating too much in the text. It makes reviewing and studying for exams difficult; students have to wade through the information to figure out what is important. Instead, successful students find ways to cut back on how much is highlighted in the text and still get a complete grasp of the topic:

- Successful students do not highlight information they already know. The best thing to do is to skim through a section to see if there is any additional information they did not already know and make a note of it.

- Successful students do not notate all of the author's examples. They jot down ideas of examples that relate to their lives. This helps them understand the information while reading and reviewing, and it helps them recall the information better in the future because it has been personalized and internalized.

- Successful students do not automatically highlight the information in the sidebars, margins, and charts. They take the time to go through the information as they go through the regular text and pull out the main points as needed.

Being selective does not mean being stingy. Some students make the mistake of not marking enough. Students who read entire sections of the book and find they have marked only one or two main ideas may want to go back and rethink about what is in the section. This is a sign they are not asking enough questions or the right questions or they have not been actively reading.

BE NEAT

It is frustrating for a student to spend an hour reading the material in a text to come back the next day and not be able to decipher his or her notes. Here are some tips to help keep books neat:

- Use pencils instead of pens so mistakes can easily be erased.

- Think carefully before highlighting or marking any of the text.

- Limit marginal notes to one sentence per paragraph.

- Write long notations on a separate sheet of paper and slip it into the book at the page it is referencing.

- Print the notes instead of using cursive.

COPY ONTO PAPER

After completing the assigned readings, successful students take the time to copy their notes and ideas from the book into their notes for several reasons. First, copying the notes, ideas, questions, and main points from the book onto paper is a way to review the reading one more time – writing the information helps ingrain it in their minds. Second, this method of reviewing allows students to organize the information in a manner that makes sense to them, such as an outline or concept map. Finally, this step in the reading process allows students to generate personal examples and connections to the real world. Here are some things to remember when copying the information from the text to the notes:

- Successful students keep trying systems and organizational methods until they find one that works for them.

- Successful students treat this process as an important study session as opposed to busywork that needs to be done before the "real studying."

- Successful students add in their own thoughts, questions, ideas, and examples during this process because this makes the information more memorable.

- Successful students highlight key words along with their definitions and explanations in their notes. One way to do this is to use the left-hand margin of the sheet to list the key words and use the body of the paper for the explanation and other information. Another method is to split the paper into three columns and put the key word or question in the left column with the explanation, answer, or definition in the middle column and the examples in the right-hand column.

MAKE CHOICES

There will be days, weeks, or semesters when the successful student cannot keep up with all of the reading for all of their classes. When this happens, it is time to make decisions. When the reading load is too heavy to keep up, the successful student must create a hierarchy of reading:

- Successful students find out which sources are favored by the professor. Doing this is as simple as looking through the syllabus to see which sources appear most often. These sources should definitely be read.

- Successful students learn to recognize how the professor refers to the reading material in class. If the professor goes over the reading material specifically, the reading can be skimmed or skipped if there is a time crunch. When skipping reading assignments, successful students reevaluate this decision on a regular basis to ensure the professor continues to thoroughly cover the material in class.

- Successful students know they can skim supplementary materials unless they are told the information will appear on the exam.

- Successful students realize when the scheduling of their courses is the main problem and they evaluate if they need to drop a class and take it later. Students can inadvertently end up with reading-intensive classes, and they may be better off taking these classes in different semesters. If this is the case, students can drop a class and take it later in their college career.

NOTE: *Dropping classes should not become a habit or a crutch for not wanting to examine reading strategies and time management skills. It is important to make several considerations before dropping a class: Is it too late to drop without getting an incomplete? Is there no way to successfully fit in all the work for these classes? Will dropping the class put the student below a full-time status, and if so what are the implications of this? Will there be a charge for dropping the class after a certain date? Is the class a prerequisite for classes the student plans on taking the following semester?*

CASE STUDY: ANGELA WESTPHAL,

Angela Westphal is an instructor at the University of Wisconsin Oshkosh. She earned her bachelor of arts from the University of Wisconsin Oshkosh in 2001. She earned a masters of arts, communication and a mediation and negotiation certificate from the University of Wisconsin Milwaukee in 2004.

Angela's thoughts on student adjustment:

The hardest adjustment seems to be learning to set the pace for your own work. I will have students tell me that they didn't know they should have been working on an assignment project "this whole time" or that they put off reading and ended up skimming all chapters the night/day/week before the exam. I believe many anticipated the specific guidance of: this week you should be this far on a project, etc. Students report difficulty in figuring out what is most important in lecture and chapters. I see this in class when I am lecturing and they will ask for specific wording over and over again. They only care about writing down what I have said, not understanding what it means or writing it in a way that makes sense. Some also try to write down everything instead of the main concepts.

CASE STUDY: ANGELA WESTPHAL,

Angela's thoughts on student surprises:

A big surprise may be that effort does not equate to quality. Students believe that if they tried hard and put effort into writing something that should count for something in the grading.

Angela's thoughts on student distractions and advice:

Students who live in the dorms seem to have a hard time balancing meeting new people and having fun with making sure course work is done. I did not even try to study in the dorms. I knew I couldn't get things done there so I wouldn't go back to my room until I was ready.

Angela's thoughts on important study tips:

You will not suddenly learn to study when classes get more difficult. Start developing effective habits your first semester in college. I post an outline online of classes and main points only. That lets them know what I think the most important parts of the chapter are and helps them pick them out on their own too. I also am a strong advocate of studying with another person.

Angela's thoughts on student challenges:

Showing up. Half of the battle is just getting to class every day and actively listening to the instructor. If you can do that consistently you are already above average.

UNDERSTANDING SUPPLEMENTARY MATERIALS

Most of the class reading comes from the assigned textbook, but there are times when professors assign supplementary reading. This could be a chapter from a different book, a newspaper or journal article, or a Web site. Whatever it is, the professor sees merit in reading it, so it is important to take it seriously.

FIGURE OUT WHY IT HAS BEEN ASSIGNED

Students sometimes get frustrated when professors assign new or unexpected readings in addition to those listed on the syllabus. One of the first things successful students do when assigned these readings is to ask the professor why this particular reading has been assigned. There are several reasons for this. First, knowing why it has been assigned can give the student the motivation to do the reading. Second, it shows the professor the student is interested in the class – as long as the question is asked with sincere curiosity. Third, it gives the student an idea of what to look for when doing the reading. Supplemental reading may be assigned for several reasons, including the following:

- To give the students greater detail or background

- To highlight specifics

- To show varying viewpoints

- To prompt a discussion or debate

- To relate real world examples

- To spark the students' interest in other facets

- To simplify a confusing section of the textbook

Do Not Dismiss Reading Strategies

Successful students follow their same reading system with supplemental readings that they follow with textbook readings. Here are more tips to help students get the most from supplemental reading assignments:

- Students need to define the author's main purpose or approach to the topic.

- Students need to consider the professor's purpose in assigning the reading so they are sure to get the right types of information from it.

- Successful students make photocopies or printouts of supplemental reading whenever possible so they can refer back to it if needed. If they cannot make a photocopy or printout of the assignment, they make the most out of their notes, even if it means taking more detailed notes than they would out of their textbook.

- Supplemental readings may contain photos, charts, graphics, and other visual items. Successful students jot down notes and information from these items as well as the readings.

GET MORE OUT OF LECTURES

Many students feel like lectures are a huge waste of time, but these students do not know the strategies necessary to get the most out of them. It is important to treat lectures seriously because professors may talk about things in the lectures that are not in the books but will be on tests. This chapter will cover the strategies successful students use before, during, and after class to help them get the information they need from the time spent in class.

READ THE CHAPTER BEFORE THE LECTURE

Successful students read the assigned reading before the lecture. This has benefits for the student:

- 📚 Students who make this process a habit get behind in the reading or have to cram before exams and quizzes.

- 📚 Students who do the reading before the class are prepared for surprise quizzes or activities.

- 📚 Students have background information about the professor's lecture. They know the vocabulary — or are at least familiar with it. They also have an idea of the main points of the lecture may be so they can anticipate what they will be listening to.

ASK A QUESTION DURING EACH CLASS PERIOD

Successful students make it a habit to ask at least one question during the class period. The key to doing this is to make sure that the questions are meaningful and related to the topic. There are reasons why this is a good idea for students:

- Asking meaningful questions shows the professor that the student is interested in the topic and listening to the lecture.

- Professors will get to know the students who are more vocal in class better than the ones who do not ask questions or participate in discussions.

- Students who know they have to ask one question during each class period will pay more attention to what the professor is saying.

- Many students think of questions while they are listening to a lecture but do not want to ask them during the class. By taking the initiative to ask one question per class period, students can get the information they need on the spot.

- Professors often leave time for questions at the end of the class or at certain points during the class. To avoid interrupting the professor, students jot down their questions in context of their notes so they do not forget what they want to ask.

Take Good Notes During Lectures

Lectures cannot be repeated, so that puts importance on getting the notes right the first time. Similar to taking notes when reading, students need to ask questions while they are listening and then listen for the answers. This is a difficult task for students, but here are some tips to help:

- Sketch out any graphs, charts, or other illustrations the professor shares during the lecture.

- Listen for signal words and phrases: "This is important." "This will be on the test." "There are three (or however many) main points."

- Find a note-taking method that works. Some students prefer to outline what the professors is saying, while others like to make lists; others like to make charts and concept maps.

- Date the notes and number the pages in case papers get mixed up. It will be easier to put them all together.

- Sit near the front of the class to force yourself to pay attention. It also helps students see the visual aids and demonstrations more clearly.

- Successful students make notations where they have further questions or where they think they may have missed something important the lecturer said. This allows them to fill in the information later.

- It is okay to stay after class and ask for clarification as long as it is a direct question about a specific part of the lecture. For example, "I think I missed the third step in the writing process, could you tell me again?" is much better than saying, "I need you to go over the writing process. I think I missed something somewhere." Students who have a specific question about a part of the lecture show they were listening and paying attention.

🕮 Successful students come prepared with ample paper and writing utensils so they are not scrambling for materials when the lecture starts.

Combine Textbook and Lecture Notes

After each lecture, successful students should take the time to go over the notes from the reading and lecture and combine them into one set of notes. There are several different methods of doing this, and the successful student needs to look at these methods and develop a system that meets his or her needs. Streamlining notes makes studying for exams and quizzes easier.

🕮 **Method #1:** Make a three-column sheet. In the first column, write the key word or concept. In the second column, reiterate what the text says about it. In the third column, add in what the professor said about it during the lecture.

🕮 **Method #2:** Combine the ideas in an outline format, paying special attention to repeat material. Material in the textbook and the lecture will likely be on the exams.

🕮 **Method #3:** Review and reflect on the material. Review both sets of notes and reflect on the main ideas. Students who do this make notes in their own words instead of copying from the two other examples.

🕮 **Method #4:** Summarize the discussed topic. Students who actively read and listen to the lecture are able to summarize the material shortly after the lecture and use the summary to recall the information when they are reviewing for exams.

BEAT THE LECTURE BLUES

Lectures, especially those in lecture halls with so many students the professor does not recognize the students' faces or know their names, can be boring and difficult to listen to at times. Successful students have found methods to reduce the tugging desire to daydream, fall asleep, or skip the lecture:

- Successful students sit near the front — every day.

- Successful students do not go to the lecture hungry. A healthy snack before the lecture can do wonders for helping with the attention span.

- Successful students do not schedule lectures during the times of day when they are least able to concentrate.

A PLAN TO COUNTERACT LECTURE DISTRACTIONS

Make a list on a separate sheet of paper and examine your attention in lecture classes by evaluating the following.

Class: List a current lecture-based class.

Problem: Identify a problem that prevents you from getting the most out of the lecture such as difficulty paying attention, missing important information in your notes, or not being able to anticipate where the professor is going with his or her lecture.

Tip: List one tip from this chapter that may help you solve your problem. Try the tip during the next week or two.

Evaluation: Write down how the tip worked for you and what steps you want to take in the future to help you achieve in this class.

CASE STUDY: CHALONDA WILLIAMS

Chalonda Williams is a senior at the University of South Carolina Upstate expecting to graduate in 2008 with a major in interdisciplinary studies focusing on political science, military science, and speech communication. She is a sergeant in the U.S. Army and plans to further her military career as well as her education by pursuing her master's degree in business administration.

Chalonda's thoughts on the learning style:

It was similar to studying in high school, just more in depth with learning and building.

Chalonda's thoughts on distractions and balancing time:

I am a mother, wife, soldier, and student so being pulled every five minutes from my studies to tend to my four-year old son is a huge distraction. I balance my time by doing my work at night.

Chalonda's thoughts on mistakes:

The biggest mistake I made was not having a better habit of studying on a regular basis. I realized it when my grades started reflecting my poor study habits.

Chalonda's thoughts on hindsight:

It was hard to learn that I didn't have to remember unnecessary things. Instead, it is important to study in relation to what type of test it will be.

Chalonda's thoughts on figuring out study tricks:

One trick is to link the information so that if you remember the key term you will remember the information that goes along with it. Another idea is to look to the end of the semester and imagine getting a good grade.

Chalonda's thoughts on routines:

One routine that works is to study on the same day of the lecture so that you can have a better memory of the information and then go back and review the information each day until the exam.

Chalonda's thoughts on obstacles:

The biggest obstacle when it comes time to study is to stick with it. Being in a place with distractions makes "attempting to study" even more difficult. To overcome this, you need to stay focused and attentive and find yourself a place where there are no distractions or disturbances.

RECOGNIZE THE IMPORTANCE OF CRITICAL THINKING

To students who have not been forced to think critically about their class material, the mention of critical thinking can be overwhelming and frightening because students may not know what it is or how to do it. Critical thinking is not a natural ability but with a few tips and tricks students can train their brains to analyze information without consciously thinking about doing it.

Critical thinking, also called evaluative thinking, refers to evaluating the material at hand and involves curiosity about the subject. Successful students who critically think about the information presented to them do not just accept the information as is. They think about it, question it, and try to take it one step further. This means they try to apply it, question its validity, or disprove it for the sake of understanding it better. Critical thinkers also look at the source to see if it is reliable or to see if it may have an underlying reason for framing the information in a certain way. All of these processes cause the successful student to better understand the information because he or she is actively using the information instead of memorizing facts.

Critical thinkers have a way of thinking that sets them apart from other people. Critical thinkers are able to impartially think about all sides of an issue and apply the evidence to any viewpoint. They are skilled at organizing ideas and can successfully articulate their thoughts. Critical thinkers are also logical and can explain why something is illogical or logical. Critical thinking allows for recognition of probable consequences before they occur.

Understand the Importance of Lateral Thinking

Edward do Bono, an expert on thinking, defines two different types of critical thinking called lateral thinking and parallel thinking. Lateral thinking is the type of thinking that aims to broaden the knowledge base through the generation of new possibilities. Successful students use lateral thinking strategies to help them find new information and to examine new viewpoints and perspectives.

Successful students use these strategies to help develop their lateral thinking skills:

- Successful students read. They read their course material, the newspaper, fiction, nonfiction, magazines, and whatever else they can find. Reading about other people's experiences, thoughts, and opinions helps the successful student have a myriad of information from which to draw new ideas.

- Successful students also feed their curiosity. Instead of skimming information or telling themselves they will find out more later, they find the answers to their questions when they are reading their texts for class or when they are reading for pleasure.

- Successful students keep running lists of "why" questions in a journal or elsewhere so they can go back and answer them when they have time. When students take a genuine interest in the world around them and unlock their curiosity, they find they have questions waiting to be answered.

- Successful students are not afraid to ask new questions and try new things such as listening to a speaker with a differing viewpoint or unfamiliar topic or by trying a new activity. New activities can change the way successful students think about familiar experiences and ideas and broaden their thinking.

- Successful students also examine the beliefs and customs of other cultures to see how other people view familiar activities and topics – and why.

UNDERSTAND THE IMPORTANCE OF PARALLEL THINKING

Parallel thinking is the thinking that makes judgments on current information. This type of thinking is what successful students use when they evaluate information because it allows them to classify and sort it.

Successful students use these strategies to help them develop their parallel thinking skills:

- List the pros and cons of each possibility.

- Look for other viewpoints during this evaluation process whether it is from friends, classmates, or professors.

- Think about the ramifications of each possibility before implementing an option.

🕮 Successful students seek advice from people who have experienced the situation before. If they are trying to figure out what a professor's first test will be like, they seek out people who have had classes with the professor before and ask about the exams.

Balance Lateral and Parallel thinking

Lateral and parallel thinking are important for successful students. They work best together. Students use lateral thinking first to generate a list of possible solutions to a problem and then move to parallel thinking to evaluate and choose the best possibility.

Here are some examples of how lateral and parallel thinking work together:

🕮 When deciding on a topic for a paper or presentation, successful students use lateral thinking to come up with a list of possible topics that fit in the assignment's parameters and then use parallel thinking to narrow it down to the best possible topic.

🕮 When answering a short answer or essay prompt on an exam, successful students think about all the possible directions they may take with the answer and then use parallel thinking to narrow it down to the best possibility.

Be Aware of Assumptions

Everyone functions on a daily basis as a result of assumptions. Successful students know, however, that it is better to critically think about what the professor may include on the exam, instead of assume it will only be information from the lecture or from the book. Otherwise they risk being grossly unprepared for the exam. Here are some ways to help avoid assumptions about studying and coursework:

- Successful students do not assume there are one or two possibilities they need to choose from. They make sure they ask questions to clarify exam questions and assignment parameters.

- Successful students fully understand the complexity and workload required for assignments before writing them off as easy or quick projects. This allows them to schedule ample time to complete the project. They do not assume it will be a quick project based on a quick glance.

- Successful students use their professor's office hours by going in for clarifications on class information and assignment directions instead of guessing or assuming they know what the professor means.

PRACTICE CRITICAL THINKING SKILLS

Successful students who understand the concepts of critical thinking take their studying a step further than those who do not. Here are some ways to do this:

- Successful students find practical applications for the material and figure out how the same ideas can be applied to different situations.

- Successful students also take advantage of assignments by thinking about the posed problems and the possible solutions before answering with the first thought that comes to mind. They evaluate the possible solutions and figure out which one is the best fit.

Successful students practice lateral thinking, parallel thinking, and assumption examination on a regular basis until it becomes a normal part of their day. After consciously doing these things, they think critically about everything without thinking about it.

Part 3

PUTTING IT ALL TOGETHER:

PROVEN TECHNIQUES FOR EXAMS

While the second part of this book explains what successful students do on a regular basis, there will be times that require specific preparation for exams. Keeping up with studies on a regular basis helps, but it is also important to have techniques ready for specific studying purposes. This section of the book aims to explain how to prepare for and take various types of exams and how to do it well.

PREPARE TO STUDY

Successful students who keep up with their studies have a much easier time preparing for exams than students who cram a month's worth (or more) of information into a night or two of studying. However, it is important to realize that different types of exams require different methods of understanding and remembering the material. Because of this, successful students take the time to question the professor about the type of exam they can expect. Professors will be candid about what types of questions they will ask. From there, successful students know how to study and prepare for the upcoming exam.

ALLOT ENOUGH TIME AND START EARLY

Students should allot eight to ten hours of study time for each test, but this number can be altered for a few reasons. Tests in classes that require a heavy load of memorization such as anatomy, geography, or foreign language will require more time. Exams that cover only one or two chapters may require less time. Students who have not kept up with daily reading assignments should allow more time to catch up. The best thing for students to do is start with about ten hours allotted. When they become accustomed to studying and if they log how long they study, they will soon be able to judge how long it will take them to study for an exam.

Ten hours sounds like a large block of time for studying — especially for students who spend one to three hours studying the night before a test. While they may find the latter method successful, it can be stressful and it does not help with retaining the knowledge for future use. Successful students understand why allotting enough time and starting early are important:

- Ten hours should be broken up into four or five smaller study sessions over the course of four or five days.

- Starting early and allotting enough time allows the successful student to prepare study materials and use a variety of study strategies to help ensure high marks on the test.

- Successful students who start early have enough time to contact the professor when they have questions about the material, when they need extra help understanding certain concepts, or if they have a hole in their notes they are unable to fill using the textbook.

- Actively study allows students to retain the information in long-term memory instead of only remembering enough to squeeze a decent grade out of the test and then forgetting much of the material.

- Cramming can be counterproductive in classes that have comprehensive exams since all of the information will need to be re-studied for each comprehensive exam. Students who rely on cramming probably just "get by" in college instead of getting the most out of the time and money they invest in their education.

ORGANIZE THE MATERIAL AND PLAN A SCHEDULE

The time allotted for studying for an exam should be carefully planned. A good way to start is to figure out as much information as possible about the test. The best way to do this is to ask the professor and students who have previously taken the class. This is not cheating; it is preparation. There are two important types of questions students ask when preparing for exams: questions about format and questions about content.

Questions to ask about the format:

- How many questions will be on the exam?

- What type of questions will be on the exam (essay, multiple choice, true or false, and others)?

- How much time will there be to complete the exam?

- Where will the testing room be? In large classes, the students may be separated into several rooms for the exam.

- Will students be required to answer all of the questions or will there be a choice of answering only a certain number of questions?

Questions to ask about the content:

- What material will be covered on the exam?

- Is there a study guide for the exam?

- Will the professor conduct a study session for the exam?

- Are there specific parts of more important information?

- What supporting materials will be covered on the exam?

When students know the above information, they can tailor their study sessions to meet these needs. Objective exams, such as multiple choice, true or false, and matching require students to know more specific details and facts, while essay exams require students to understand broader concepts and how they apply to situations.

When planning a study schedule, successful students start four or five days before the day of the exam. The first study session should be spent organizing the materials and the next three or four sessions should be spent studying the materials using a variety of study methods. Successful students have found these tips to be helpful when figuring out how and when to study:

- 📚 Organize and prepare study materials. Set a time limit or it is easy to put off studying by organizing, re-reading, outlining, and re-outlining material instead of actively studying it.

- 📚 View the planning and organizing stage as a valid study session. It should not be done in front of the television or while visiting with friends. When taken seriously, the planning stage can help familiarize the student with the information.

- 📚 Students use the organization time to determine which main points need to be studied and then find the notes from lectures and other materials that go with each main point.

- 📚 The planning session is a time to develop study sheets such as concept maps, note cards, questions, outlines, and tests and to answer the study guide questions and predict essay exam questions that will be used later in the study schedule. The planning session also requires the student to block out time each day to study the materials and lists what will be studied each day. Some students like to study one section of the material each day, while others prefer to study all the material using a different method each day.

- 📚 Successful students realize the importance of not planning a study session immediately preceding the exam. They know it helps the brain to get ready for the exam to do something relaxing such as listening to music, visiting with friends, going for a walk, or doing anything else fun to give the brain time to think about the information without cramming.

PREDICT QUESTIONS

Students may find themselves in a class where the professor gives them a list of the questions that will be on the exam. The list may be definitive in that it is a copy of the exam or it may be a database of questions from which the professor will pull questions. It may be a list of questions similar to the questions on the exam. Students with these resources have one important step completed for them because they know what to study.

An effective way to prepare the material for study sessions is to predict which questions will be on the exam. Successful students find that predicting about four or five times the number of questions that will be on the actual exam is a good number. These questions and their answers can be used to create study materials for study sessions.

Before predicting questions, it is important to know what types of questions to ask. For objective tests, questions should be specific and include definitions, dates, people, key concepts, and formulas. Anything bold, highlighted, or in the margins of the textbook as well as main points in the lecture notes is a good place to start. Another place to find information is in the key terms at the end of the chapters or suggested during lectures. Subjective, or essay, exams focus more on general topics. These questions can be made from the main points in the lecture and textbook but also focus on application from the questions and may require the students to tie together two or more main points. Predicted subjective questions should emulate this.

It also helps to think about the specific subject when trying to predict questions.

Math

While objective questions on math exams may require the student to demonstrate the usage of learned formulas, there will be other objective questions relating to mathematicians and theory:

> 📚 Who first discovered . . . ?

> 📚 Why was "X" finally discounted?

> 📚 When is "X" not the best formula to use for . . . ?

Math exams may also contain subjective questions:

> 📚 Explain why it is it important to . . .

> 📚 Outline the theory behind . . .

> 📚 Give three examples of how "X" could be used to . . .

Social Sciences

History, geography, psychology, sociology, and philosophy classes allow for a wide range of objective and subjective questions. Some common types of objective questions are:

> 📚 What date did . . . ?

> 📚 Who was the first person to . . . ?

> 📚 Why did . . . ?

❧ What is . . . ?

❧ The best definition of "X" is . . . ?

❧ Which of the following is the biggest effect of . . . ?

❧ The result of "X" was . . .

❧ What do experts believe is the cause of . . . ?

❧ Which happened first . . . ?

Common subjective questions for social sciences include:

❧ Trace the events leading up to . . .

❧ Compare and contrast two events, people, theories, or concepts . . .

❧ Explain the causes or effects of . . .

❧ What is the relationship between . . . ?

❧ Apply "X" theory to your own life . . .

❧ Explain why someone would choose "X" over "Y" . . .

Language

Whether the class is a foreign language or an English class, it will either focus on usage (such as vocabulary and grammar) or literature (including historical and cultural accounts). Objective tests for language classes may include questions about vocabulary, definitions, proper usage, and grammar. The questions for literature classes focus on comprehension, including key events, characters or people, the order of events, and the effects of events.

Subjective tests delve further. Foreign language tests can have similar questions as social sciences about history and culture. Literature classes may ask students to:

- Analyze a certain aspect of a reading

- Compare and contrast two characters or concepts in a reading or in two separate readings

- Apply or trace events

- Explain how they would have reacted if they were a character in the story

Science

Objective questions deal with definitions, dates, theories, concepts, hypothesis, and experiments. Subjective questions may ask the students to:

- Explain a process

- Apply a hypothesis

- Compare theories

- Contrast concepts

- Trace events leading up to a discovery

USE PROVIDED RESOURCES

Students may arrive at college with the preconceived notion that they are on their own. What they do not realize is colleges and universities, while learning institutions at heart, are also "businesses" in the sense that they need to succeed to stay afloat. The best way to prove success for colleges and universities is to promote the success of their students. They know they cannot give A's to every student, so they create a plethora of resources for students to help them earn successful grades.

The first thing successful students do is find out what study help resources are available. These can be found by visiting the dean of students office, the library, the advising center, or the student information office. These resources include the following:

> **Writing Centers.** English majors and English graduate students staff the writing centers as writing tutors. Students can go to the writing center for help throughout the writing process or with a draft for review.

> **Testing Review Rooms.** Universities may have a room, perhaps in the library, which contains files of old tests from professors. Students can find the tests from their professors and use the tests as study guides.

> **Tutor Labs.** Universities offer tutor labs where students can sign up for tutor sessions. They are paired with majors and graduate students to help them through the information and are flexible in terms of the number of meetings per week and times of the sessions.

Other resources for students are those offered by the professor. Anytime a professor says, "This is important!" or "This will be on the exam!" he or she is giving the students a sneak peek at what information will be required for the exam. Other things professors may offer to students for help:

> **Study Sessions.** Professors may schedule a study session in the evening the night before or a few nights before an exam. Students are allowed to come with questions and sometimes the professor will go over key concepts that will appear on the exam.

📖 **Study Groups.** Some professors organize study groups or set up a time and place for interested students to meet to study for an exam.

📖 **Study Guides.** Professors may hand out study guides that list the information needed to do well on the exam. Students should study all of the information on the guide since it will likely appear on the exam.

Successful students learn how to create their own study guides. Previous assignments, review questions, and quizzes can help students ascertain what will be on the exam.

Finally, successful students inquire in the library for resources for certain topics. The library media center may have computer programs or links to Internet sites that contain practice tests for entry level general education subjects. While these practice tests may not be written specifically by the professor, if they cover the information offered in the classes they will be helpful — if only as a review the day before the test.

CASE STUDY: ANDREA QUENETTE

Andrea Quenette graduated from North Dakota State University with a bachelor's degree in mass communication and psychology and a master's degree in mass communication.

Andrea's thoughts on the learning style:

College learning demands your time. You have to commit specific time to do that and it trades off with other activities. I was surprised I could remember a lot and do very well on an exam or quiz, but I didn't retain all of the information later. This hurt me in classes like French where retention and memory are important. I found that I could memorize the vocabulary words and their translations and then complete the exam. The problem was I could not remember any of the words I supposedly "learned" later when I was expected to use them.

CASE STUDY: ANDREA QUENETTE

Andrea's thoughts on directions and balancing time:

Friends, work, family – they are all distractions. I learned to spend time studying with my friends. We brought our books and stuff over to each other's houses and worked in the same room. Work was difficult to balance with studying. I was fortunate to find a job where I was able to study while I was working.

Andrea's thoughts on mistakes:

I could do very well on an exam or quiz, but I didn't always retain all of the information later.

Andrea's thoughts on hindsight:

For certain classes I don't know that my methods were that beneficial to me. I would have liked a little more guidance for those classes that were beyond notes, lectures, textbook readings, etc. For example, I still feel incompetent in my ability to speak French even though I spent 5 years studying it. I did well on the exams, assignments and speaking situations but I don't feel that I can actually speak French.

Andrea's thoughts on figuring out study tricks:

Repetition. Whether it is notes or vocabulary I read, re-read, and recite to myself the terms or concepts that I need to know until I have committed them to memory. Also, spend more time reviewing the newer material as you haven't spent as much time using the ideas.

Andrea's thoughts on challenges:

The biggest challenge for college students is remembering that when you enroll, you are paying money and you need to commit to school as though it were a job. Your boss doesn't let you miss your shift because you had to be somewhere trivial or overslept. You need to go to class every day and read the textbook.

Andrea's thoughts on routines:

I read the textbook every class period. That way as we learn it in class I can reinforce it with the book. Then, when the test is coming up, I plan two or three days in advance

CASE STUDY: ANDREA QUENETTE

where I concentrate on reviewing all of my notes and finishing up my reading in the book. I take the instructor's study guide (if they give one) and write down all the ideas and concepts that relate to the terms or phrases they give us. I think about the information I might be asked to reflect in the exam. After two or three days of reviewing the material, I felt pretty confident.

Andrea's thoughts on obstacles:

You also have to make it a commitment. There are times in graduate school where I just didn't have time to read the textbook or outside readings and I don't feel that I served myself effectively. If your friends aren't busy and want you to do something, it is easy to push aside your books and go have a good time. Although I think you have to learn from experience what your needs and boundaries are, I had to learn to stick to my guns and be firm about the time I needed to study. I learned how to fit that time into other parts of my day so I could make time for friends too.

ACTIVE STUDYING STRATEGIES

Simply reading and rereading notes is not enough for successful students. To get to know and understand the information, successful students find active studying strategies to be successful. While students find a few of these strategies that they like the best, it is also important to remember that successful students use two or three different strategies when studying for each test to help them remember the information better and to be able to recall the information more easily when under the pressure of the actual exam.

SUMMARIZE AND CONDENSE

Summarizing and condensing works for subjective exams requires students to have a good knowledge of the information and to be able to recall it and apply it but does not require the students to remember specific dates, numbers, or definitions. Throughout this process students put the information into their own words and restate it several times to help them understand the concepts and main points. The students continue summarizing and condensing the information until they are able to use a basic key word study sheet to help them recall the information. Here is how it is done:

One consideration for making these sheets — if the test is strictly essay questions and the professor provides a list of possible essay questions — is each sheet should cover one essay question. The information the student adds to the sheet should be the answer to the question.

At this point, the preparation work for this type of active studying is complete. There are several ways to use the sheets, but the basic premise is that the students read and review the sheets until they can remember enough of the information to condense it down one step. If it is a three-step outline, they can rewrite the outline leaving out the third step but recalling the information when looking at the outline. If it is paragraph, they condense the paragraph into fewer sentences. They continue to condense the information until all they have left is a basic form of the original that still has the key words. As they review this basic sheet they can recall the details related to each key word.

Here is an example of how this works:

BOOK EXCERPT

(From *101 Businesses You Can Start With Less Than One Thousand Dollars: For Students* by Heather Shepard.)

Health Care for the Self-employed

Health care can be a major expense, especially when you are on your own. Here are some options for those just getting their business off the ground to consider.

First. You can get free health care through your county's jobs and family service center. Your local jobs and family service centers can give you and your family full coverage insurance depending on how much your current family income is. You should contact your local jobs and family service center to see if you are eligible for this practical benefit.

Second. You can locate a health clinic that accepts payment on a sliding scale. There are a number of clinics that use a sliding scale for the use of their services. They take into account your current income and adjust it to how much you can afford. This

BOOK EXCERPT

could come out to you paying anywhere from zero to 100 percent. Normally these clinics are found in your local phone book. This also applies to many clinical dental offices as well.

Third. You can become a member of low-cost health care options with your state or local government. You can contact your local health department to obtain information on local government or national government programs for working families. The benefits are unlimited and include complete dental, medical, eye, and prescription services for a low fee. Eligibility depends on your family size and current income ratio.

Fourth. Membership groups, such as small business and the type of industry you are affiliated with (writers, media, and so on) all offer their members low cost health insurance.

One thing hospitals may not disclose is that you can also receive emergency visits on a sliding scale. If you have an emergency visit or are forced to have unforeseen surgery and are currently without health care coverage, you can ask for an H-CAP application. How much you pay will be on a family size to current income ratio. This program may pay off the entire hospital bill.

Summary #1:

There are four ways to find affordable health care for self-employed business owners.

1. The first way is to look into the county's jobs and family service center which may provide insurance at a rate determined by the family's income. It requires an application and is only available to eligible families.

2. The second way is to look for health clinics that charge for services on a sliding scale based on the patient's or family's income. Based on current income, people pay a percentage of the original cost of the service or treatment. This is also an option for dental care.

3. The third way is to look into state and local government programs

for working families may include dental, eye, and medical care. Families need to apply and be eligible for such programs.

4. The fourth way is to look into health insurance offered to members of professional groups. This insurance is at a lower cost than if they purchased the insurance independently.

Summary #2:

There are four ways to find affordable health care

1. Look for county programs through the jobs and family service center to see if the family's income makes them eligible.

2. Find health clinics that offer services on a sliding percentage scale based on the family's income.

3. Utilize state and local government programs to determine eligibility for dental, eye, and medical care programs.

4. Investigate health insurance options with professional membership groups.

Summary #3:

4 ways to find affordable health care:

1. County jobs and family services center

2. Health clinics with sliding scales

3. Local and state government programs

4. Professional membership groups

Students who use this method find different ways to implement the process:

USE FLASH CARDS

Creating flash cards is another way for students to study material for objective exams. Flash cards are portable and successful study aids for all subjects. They can be saved to use for studying and reviewing for comprehensive exams later in the semester. Here are some examples:

SUBJECT	SIDE 1	SIDE 2
History	Person's Name	Significance
	Date	Events
	Name of a Battle	Details
	Name of an Era	Details/description
Science	Keyword	Definition
	Sketch	Description
	Name of a process	Process
	Element	Description
Literature	Character	Description
	Author	Name of Works
	Title	Outline of Plot
	Keywords	Definitions
	Act or Scene Number	Outline of Events
Foreign Language	Foreign Word	English Word
	Grammar Rule	Example
	Verb	Conjugation
	Historical Dates	Significance

Successful students offer the following tips when using flashcards to study:

Use Visual Depictions of Information

Visual depictions of the information can be helpful study aids for both subjective and objective tests. The options for these depictions include maps, time lines, charts, graphs, diagrams, and cluster maps. Similar to the two previous methods, the information on the visual depictions should be grouped by main point or concept if they are being used to cover all of the information to be studied.

Visual depictions do not need to cover all of the information if the students use them along with another active study method. For example, a time line may be appropriate to help a student remember the details of part of a larger event. Students can also use visual depictions to help them tie the main points together such as trying to figure out how seemingly unrelated historical events led up to one significant historical event through the use of a cluster map.

Successful students use these visual depictions in many different ways to aide in their studying. They can:

CREATE A STUDY GROUP

Successful students know study groups can be one of the largest assets when it comes to study aids, but they can also be the biggest downfall for students who do not know how to use them correctly. Here are some helpful hints that successful students use to make study groups work for them:

Master the Review

Last-chance review sessions are an important opportunity for successful students. They have prepared their study materials and spent several study sessions actively studying the material. The last study session before the test should be a review instead of trying to cram in more information which may stress the brain.

These review sessions should not occur immediately before the class but can occur the night before or earlier in the day. There are many different ways to review.

Whatever method successful students use, they make sure they have gone over all of the information one last time and they do not use this time to try to learn new information. The review session should be proof to students that they know the information and are prepared for the upcoming exam.

PLAN A TEST-TAKING STRATEGY

Actively studying is the best way to prepare for an exam, but it is also important for students to know what to do and expect when they get to the exam. For some students, exam time is a time of anxiety to the point that even though they know the information they are unable to express it on the exam. Other students find themselves making careless mistakes that cost them valuable points. Successful students know good strategies can be applied to all test-taking situations to help them relax as well as stop losing points for careless reasons.

OVERCOME TEST ANXIETY

Test anxiety is not only normal, it is also necessary for students to take the time to prepare for the exam. If there were no anxiety, they would not feel the need to prepare for the exam. Text anxiety manifests itself in varying degrees of physical and mental symptoms including sweating, nausea, headaches, butterflies, forgetfulness, worry, lack of concentration, and physical and mental tensing. Successful students, even those who experience extreme text anxiety, have found ways to overcome these potentially debilitating symptoms:

Prepare and study.

Practice relaxation techniques such as taking deep breaths and slowly exhaling or purposefully tensing and relaxing muscles.

Recite positive statements before and during the exam such as: "I can do this," "I am relaxed," and "I am prepared; I know the information."

Monitor the timing. Successful students determine if it is better to get to the exam site early or right on time. This is different for everyone because some people who arrive early get all worked up about the exam while others need that extra time to relax and focus.

Arrive prepared. Successful students have used the restroom and dressed appropriately so they are not too cold or too warm. They also have plenty of writing utensils and paper to get them through the exam.

RESIST THE URGE

It happens in classrooms right before an exam. Students are talking about the information and asking each other for help or advice. They are cramming more information into their brains. Successful students resist the urge to partake in or listen to these conversations because:

They know they have studied and know the information.

They do not want to get information from other students that may not be accurate.

- They do not want to try to cram any more new information into their brains.

- They have relaxed for a while before the exam so they do not want to start working their brains until the exam starts.

READ DIRECTIONS

Successful students take a few minutes to look over the exam and get a feel of what is expected of them. They skim over the questions and read the directions and underline or circle key words. Sometimes a test section may seem self-explanatory, but the professor may have made a few notes in the directions that, if not followed, can cost the student valuable points. These directions may include:

- Choosing all of the correct answers on multiple choice.

- Choosing only the incorrect answer on multiple choice.

- Using all of the options on matching even if some terms have more than one answer.

- Correcting false statements on true or false sections.

- Only completing a certain number of questions.

SET PRIORITIES AND BUDGET TIME

Professors may only allow students the regular class time to finish an exam. Because of this, successful students have found ways to set priorities and budget their time to ensure they have enough time to finish the exam. They allow themselves to make a game plan for the first few minutes (no more than five) before starting to answer questions.

Successful students first decide which questions to do first and which ones to leave until the end:

- Successful students go through the entire exam and answer all of the questions they know first and then go back to work on the rest.

- Successful students complete the types of questions they like the best first and leave the types of questions they least like for last.

- Successful students complete the questions worth the most points first and do the questions worth the least points last.

Second, successful students develop their own methods on how to budget their time. One way to stay on this time budget is to make notes on the test indicating the time they need to be done with each section.

- Successful students set a certain amount of time per question or per page based on the number of questions per page.

- Successful students use the formula that the percentage of points equals the percentage of time. So, if the student has 50 minutes to complete the 100-point test, each point can take 30 seconds or a five point questions can take two and a half minutes. This sounds complicated, but successful students who use this method know if all of the questions are worth two points except for the essay which is worth 20 points, they can spend ten minutes on the essay and 40 minutes on the rest of the test as a whole.

- Successful students know if they want to make sure they finish an exam in time, they skip questions they are struggling with and go back to work on them at the end. Another benefit to doing this is they may read a different question that will jog their memory enough to find the answer to the question they were not sure about. Other questions may also provide clues to at least rule out some possible answers and narrow down the list of possible correct answers.

USE EVERY SECOND

Successful students budget time to review the exam before handing it in to the professor — the professor is not going to give extra points to the students who finish early, so it is okay to use extra time to review the exam.

Some students read this section and shake their heads because they are firm believers in sticking with their first instinct when it comes to answering exam questions. This is absolutely true. When reviewing a test, successful students know in the majority of cases, the only time they should change an answer is if they found information on another part of the test that led them to the correct answer.

Here are some exceptions to that rule that makes reviewing a vital step in successful exam taking:

- Successful students read the directions again to make sure they were followed accordingly.

- Successful students double check answer sheets to make sure the answers are in the correct spots.

- Successful students look for spelling, grammar, and editing errors in essays and short answers.

- Successful students spend time looking over questions that require complex answers to make sure they did not skip a step or miss an important point.

- Successful students ask themselves if the answer makes sense in relation to the question.

TAKING THE OBJECTIVE EXAM

One of the biggest advantages of the objective exam is objective questions do not require the student to have total recall of the information, just the ability to recognize accurate information. The downfall for students is when the facts they remember are hazy and the offered possible answers are confusing.

MAKE THE RIGHT CHOICE

When completing multiple choice exams, successful students develop a plan. First they look over all the questions and answer the ones they know. Then they work on the remaining questions. Here are some hints that successful students use to help them get past the difficult questions they encounter:

Example Question: The first step in successfully taking an exam is to:

    A. The key words.
    B. Answer the easy questions first.
    C. Budget the time.
    D. Read the directions.
    E. All of the above.

- **Look for grammatical errors.** If the possible answer does not grammatically match up with the stem, then it can be discarded as a correct answer. For example, "A" does not grammatically fit with the stem so it can be thrown out.

- **Read all possibilities.** There may be a good answer to the question and a better answer to the question. In the above example a student may read "B" and think it is a good answer. However, "D" is the best answer because students need to read the directions before they know how to answer even the easy questions correctly.

- **Underline key words and phrases.** This helps the student focus on the details that may eliminate some answers. In the above question, students should underline "first step" to help them focus.

- **Make statements.** Another tip successful students use on difficult multiple choice questions is to make the question and each possible answer into a statement and then determine if the statement is true or false. The ones they know are false can be eliminated. In the above example the statements would be:

    A. The first step in successfully taking an exam is to the key words.

    B. The first step in successfully taking an exam is to answer the easy questions first.

    C. The first step in successfully taking an exam is to budget the time.

    D. The first step in successfully taking an exam is to read the directions.

- **Answer before looking.** Some successful students try to answer the question before looking at the alternatives so they do not confuse themselves with the distracters.

📖 Deal with "all of the above." This answer can be eliminated if there is one answer students know is wrong. Likewise, if two possible answers are right, it is likely the correct answer is "all of the above" even if the student is unsure about the remaining options. Students can apply the same logic to "none of the above" options.

📖 When all else fails, guess. Successful students know leaving a question blank is a way to get zero points, but putting an answer in the blank, even if it is a guess, is better than nothing.

FIND THE TRUTH

True or false questions can stump students because they find themselves second-guessing their first instinct. Here are some hints and tips to help get through these test sections.

📖 Successful students know the entire statement must be true for the answer to be true. If there is one word that makes the statement false or even partially false, then the answer has to be false.

📖 Successful students underline key words and phrases in true or false statements to help them look for parts of the statement that may be false. Some examples of important key words include names, dates, numbers, places, and titles.

📖 Successful students are aware that absolute words such as "always," "none," "only," and "never" may render the statement false because there may be exceptions to the rule.

📖 Successful students are aware qualifying words such as "some," "usually," "often," "may," "many," and "can" render an otherwise false statement true because they leave room for exceptions.

- ❧ Successful students look for a word or an omission of a word that makes the statement false.

- ❧ Successful students correct the false statements if they have time so they remember why they marked them false in the first place. This is a way to show the professor why they marked the statement as they did in case there is a question later.

- ❧ Successful students know when they have to guess they should put "true" because professors may make more true statements than false statements.

PLAY MATCHMAKER

Matching tests seem straightforward and easy, but they can take a turn for the worse with one wrong answer. This is because students make their choices and cross off the used options. If one of these options is wrong, it can throw off all of the following answers or require substantial reworking to fix mistakes. There is nothing more frustrating for students working to finish an exam on time than having to erase all the answers and markings and start from scratch in a matching section. Successful students use the following tips to help them quickly and efficiently get through the matching sections on exams:

- ❧ Working from the side with the most words can be faster because students have fewer words to scan when looking for the correct "match."

- ❧ The best way to start is to make one pass through all of the options and only mark the answers the student knows with certainty. This will eliminate a number of options.

🐚 Students should continue to go through and mark answers that can be made with certainty based on which options are left. The second pass will yield a few more answers based on the eliminated options from the first time and so on for each pass through all of the remaining options.

🐚 If students get to a point where they cannot make any more certain answers, then it is time to eliminate the incorrect possibilities. After that, students should guess.

TAKING THE ESSAY EXAM

Essay exams require a different type of knowledge than objective exams because essay exams ask the student to apply information. This means the student must have a deeper understanding of the information and how the different concepts and main points relate to each other.

Successful students know the first step in completing an essay exam is to carefully read the directions. This will tell them how many questions to answer, how long the answers should be, what extra information must be turned in such as outlines and notes, and what format the students should use such as writing only on one side of the paper or skipping lines. Successful students know it is important to analyze the questions to make sure they have a good understanding of what is being asked of them. Students can read the chapter in the next section called "Understanding Directive Words" to help them decode the essay exam questions.

Successful students also:

- Refrain from answering more than the assigned number of questions. This allows them to focus their energy on the number that will be graded.

- Look for clues when there is not a specified length. Essay or short answer questions that only leave one-third or one-quarter of the page are not asking for more than a few sentences for an answer. Questions that have one or more pages are looking for longer, more in-depth answers.

- Read through all of the questions before starting to answer them so they can choose the questions they are most prepared to answer.

- Plan with a short outline and a few notes before beginning any writing.

- Avoid a rough draft since there is rarely time to rewrite a final draft. They take the necessary steps to ensure proper organization and neatness the first time through.

- Do not discard their experience with the writing process. They may condense the steps, but they are all there. This means they create a thesis statement, write an outline, and draft the essay. If there is time they do a quick editing session to catch any major errors.

- Answer the questions instead of simply writing down all of the information they know about the topic.

- Keep the essay neat and easy to read by using margins, neat penmanship, and blue or black ink unless something else is specified in the directions.

Above all, successful students make sure they turn in well-written, focused, organized, and well-thought writing.

TAKING THE OPEN BOOK EXAM

Open book exams, a variation on traditional essay exams, sound easy. Mention of an open book exam can be a code word for students not to study for an exam. This is a grave mistake. Open book exams can be more difficult than traditional exams and are meant to test the students' ability to use, apply, and think about the information instead of the students' ability to memorize and repeat facts. Open book exams require critical thinking and the ability to construct and support arguments with facts and expert opinion.

Preparation is key when it comes to open book exams. Students need to know the material and where to find the facts they need to back up their arguments, opinions, and use of the key concepts. One possible way to study for an open book exam is to create study sheets similar to the summarizing and condensing activity. It is not as necessary to memorize the information as it is to be familiar with it and know how to apply it.

Before going to an open book exam, successful students get clear notes from the professor about what they are and are not allowed to bring to the test. Some professors put no limits, while others only allow one notebook or textbook, or students may only bring in a specific number of sheets of paper filled with notes.

Open book exams can be overwhelming for students who have not experienced them, but here are some tips for successful students:

 Less is more. It is possible to bring too much information into the test. The test may be timed so there is not enough time to go through piles of resources. This is where preparation helps. One or two textbooks and well-thought notes are key.

 Make a cheat sheet. Students who are allowed to bring in their own notes find it useful to have a cheat sheet of main points, important dates, key formulas, or other relevant information for quick access during the exam.

 Read carefully. This includes directions and exam questions. The directions will give information on the required format of the exam, while the questions will explain the type of information requested. Students should refer to the "Understanding Directive Words" chapter for more information on how to answer specific types of questions.

 Quote the experts. When answering the essay questions, successful students quote the book and other experts covered in class materials to back up their answers, but they also know the professor is not looking for an answer copied right out of the book so they include their own ideas, opinions, and analysis.

 Put main focus on content. Some students struggle with answering essay questions because they are perfectionists when it comes to writing. This is a difficult habit to break, but with time constraints present in open book exams, successful students put priority on content and worry about style later. This does not mean they disregard all of their writing skills; it means they do not have to write a stellar metaphor when a plain comparison does the trick.

Another example is using a regular word instead of taking the time to look up the "perfect" word in a thesaurus.

Know when to stop. Open book exams may be designed with limits – either page limits, time limits, or both. This means students need to be able to state their answers concisely and accurately.

There is another less common type of open book exam. These exams are take-home exams where the professor assigns the questions and gives the students a certain amount of time outside class to complete the answer. These tests do not require as much preparation before the exam, but they do require a thorough use of materials to answer the posed question.

REVIEW RETURNED TESTS

Upon leaving the classroom after an exam, students try to forget about the exam as soon as possible. Other than looking at the number grade they ignore the scored exam. They do not realize they are forgoing an easy task that can be successful practice to help them improve their grade or ensure continued success on future exams in the class: Successful students take an hour or two to review all of their returned tests and to analyze how well their study methods worked and or failed.

LOOK AT MISTAKES

Successful students take the time to go over their mistakes. They do this for a few reasons. First, it helps them note the types of information they either did not study or studied incorrectly. It also helps them see if they need help mastering a certain concept before moving on to something new in the course. Looking at the mistakes also helps students see if they made careless errors or if they misread the directions. Since professors tend to find an exam style and stick with it, this review of errors will help when taking future exams. Finally, going over the mistakes helps students see the type of information the professor looks for, especially on short answer and essay questions.

🐛 Successful students go one step further and take the time to find out and understand the correct answer. If they cannot figure out the right answer or understand why their answer was wrong, they go to the professor for an explanation and help in understanding the correct answer.

🐛 Successful students also look for the right answer in notes from the text and lectures to check their note-taking accuracy. If they studied their notes and the information was wrong in the notes, then they know to do more careful note taking in the future.

🐛 Successful students make notes of the areas of information they missed on the exam so they know what needs to be relearned instead of just reviewed for comprehensive exams later in the semester.

READ AND UNDERSTAND COMMENTS

Successful students make sure they can read and understand the comments written on the exam. If they cannot read or do not understand the instructor's comments, they plan to visit the professor for clarification. This is important because these comments give insight on the types of information the professor looks for and help the students know what to include in the future:

🐛 Comments that say, "You might have . . ." mean, "You should have . . ." or, "In the future you may try . . ." means, "In the future you should try . . ."

🐛 Professors also comment on the use of details by telling when and where students need more details and when and where they need to be more general in their answers.

🐛 They also may point out patterns in errors such as, "It looks like you might be confusing X and Y by the way you are answering these questions."

 Professors may not understand a student's answers and may make a request to see the student to discuss it. They will not try to track the student down to have this discussion but will leave it up to the student to find the them and initiate the discussion.

Professors also make comments about the format of the exam and on the students' test-taking procedures that will help the students evaluate and alter their testing strategies for the next test:

 A comment on a test that says the professor could not read the student's handwriting is a clue to the student to slow down and be neat.

 Comments may point out an error in how the student followed directions, and since professors tend to use the same basic format for all tests this helps the student know what to look for in the future.

 Professors may also give the students hints on which parts of the test to focus on first if the test was not completed in the time allotted.

Professors will also write comments about the students' test-taking method or obvious patterns. For essay exams they may comment on the support or format of the answer.

CREATE A STUDY LOG

Successful students keep a study log for each class. The log includes how long they studied for the exam and their grade. Other information included in the log is:

- Whether most of the questions came from the assigned reading or from the lecture

- What types of problems were troublesome so they can work on strategies for these types of problems

- Comments from the professor to help the students evaluate their test taking strategies

- Specific parts of the information that were studied incorrectly or insufficiently

Part 4

COMPLETING
ASSIGNMENTS

While individual, regular reading assignments and study guide or review questions are rarely graded in college-level courses, students are required to complete papers, presentations, or projects. Because there are few smaller assignments to go along with them, these larger assignments may make up a large percentage of a student's grade in the class, so it is important they understand the assignment and have a strategy in place to complete the assignment effectively.

DIRECTIVE WORDS & PHRASES

Many students struggle with assignments because they do not understand what they are supposed to do. They may see the topic in the project description and spend their time gathering information about the topic. Then they try to cram as much information as possible into the space or time allotted. The problem is they fail to take the time to understand what the professor is asking them to do with the information.

Professors ask students to use the information they have researched in a specific way. This request may be in the assignment description in the form of directive words and phrases. Successful students know how to decode these directive words and phrases so they can understand the type of project they are to complete, the type of information they are to include, and the type of approach they should take to complete the project.

Take the topic of "learning styles" for example. Some students will look at a prompt and see the key words "learning styles" and write everything they know about learning styles. This is not the best approach. Successful students know there are other key words in the assignment prompt and use them together to formulate their assignment.

Decipher Level One Directive Words

Level One directive words require the student to give information about a specific topic. This type of project requires research for facts and rarely asks for analysis, interpretation, or opinions of the topic. Successful students approach these types of projects as if they are a reporter looking for all of the information and report "just the facts" of who, what, where, when, how, and why.

Describe

Assignments requesting the students to "describe" want them to write a detailed description of the topic. These assignments should follow a logical sequence and should use plenty of examples to "show" the professor or audience what they are describing.

Example: Choose and describe five learning styles.

- 🕮 **Key words:** The key words are "five" and "describe".

- 🕮 **Description:** Successful students choose their topics and write about them in a way that "shows" the professor or other audience what each learning style is using examples. They may describe the characteristics of people who prefer the learning style, in what situations the learning style is useful, and in what situations the learning style has proven to be problematic.

- 🕮 **Warnings:** The assignment prompt is not asking students to judge or evaluate the learning styles.

- 🕮 **Format:** Unless otherwise noted, "describe" assignments may look for answers in paragraph form.

Research

Assignments requesting the students to "research" are telling the students to go beyond the information presented in class and found in the assigned readings. The professor wants students to dig deeper to get a more thorough understanding of the topic.

Example: Research the implications of not determining and developing a preferred learning style.

- **Key words:** The key words are "research," "implications," and "not."

- **Description:** Successful students know they are looking for specific information about a learning style of their choice. They must look for examples that describe what happens to students who do not know their preferred learning style and how to use it to their advantage.

- **Warnings:** Some students may not carefully read the prompt and miss the "not" in the directions. Other students may spend a good portion of the assignment describing the chosen learning style, but the prompt says to write about the implications so the students should assume the audience knows what the learning styles are.

- **Format:** The format is not noted in this instance. Answers to research prompts can be listed, written in paragraph form, or diagrammed. Students who are unsure should consult with the professor for further details.

State

Assignments requesting the students to "state" the information are looking for a recollection of information. These prompts require brief answers with few details other than the key words or phrases requested.

Example: State the ten learning styles discussed in class.

- **Key words:** The key words in this prompt are "state," "ten," and "in class."

- **Description:** Successful students know they need to think about what learning styles were presented during lectures and class discussions and write them down.

- **Warnings:** The key word "in class" shows students there may be different learning styles presented in the book but the professor is looking for the ones mentioned in class. While some students may write down all of the learning styles they can think of, they need to differentiate between which ones were presented in class and which ones were presented elsewhere.

- **Format:** This prompt asks for a simple list void of details, examples, or descriptions.

Define

Assignments requesting the students to "define" are asking students to give the topic's meaning according to someone or a specific source. The source may be specified. When it is not specified, successful students know to look for information in a few sources to find the most accurate definition possible.

Example: Define three learning styles based on the information given in the text.

- **Key words:** The key words are "define," "three," "learning styles," and "text."

- **Description:** Successful students know they need to go to the text to find the information needed to complete this assignment. They look over the information and devise their own definition based on what the book says.

🕮 **Warnings:** Some students may copy the information from a source, but the professor is looking for them to define the requested terms in their own words. Successful students know that to define a term in their own words they need to understand it first.

🕮 **Format:** The prompt to define a term means the answer will be only a few sentences. There are cases, however, where the professor asks the term be defined in a longer format. In such cases, students should look for various ways to define a term including breaking the topic into smaller sections and defining each individual section.

Explain a Process

Assignments requesting the students to "explain a process" are similar to the "describe" and "define" prompts. Successful students know explaining a process requires them to look at all aspects of the topic and give full details for each one organizing them in a sequential manner.

Example: Explain the process of determining a learning style.

🕮 **Key words:** The key words are "explain," "process," and "learning style."

🕮 **Description:** Successful students complete this assignment by first finding information about the steps to determine a learning style and then giving details and examples for each step.

🕮 **Warnings:** Students may think listing the steps is enough, but listing the steps and explaining the background, examples, and possible road blocks for each step gives more explanation than a simple, one sentence step.

> **Format:** The assignments for explaining a process can be written in a step-by-step list as long as the steps include explanations. Some professors may require that the information be written out in paragraph form; however, this means each step would be a paragraph in the finish project.

Enumerate/List

Assignments requesting the students to "enumerate" or "list" want them to recall key words, examples, or steps in a process. These types of assignments are not looking for long explanations of the items in the list, only the basic information.

Example: List the steps a student should use to determine their learning style.

> **Key words:** The key words are "list," "steps," and "learning style."

> **Description:** Successful students know they need to recall, locate, or determine the steps students should take when they want to know what learning styles they prefer. They also know they do not need to describe the steps, but list them accordingly.

> **Warnings:** Some students do not take a listing prompt seriously because it sounds easy and straightforward. For the most part, it is straightforward, but students need to ensure they list all of the necessary points.

> **Format:** This assignment should be presented in a numerical list. If it is a process, the items should be listed chronologically.

Summarize

Assignments requesting the students to "summarize" want them to take a large amount of information and condense it in their own words. This shows the professor they understand the material enough to write it in their own words and they are able to pick out the most important points.

Example: Summarize the characteristics of three different learning styles.

- **Key words:** The key words are "summarize," "three," and "learning styles."

- **Description:** Successful students choose three of the given learning styles and summarize their characteristics. To do this, they pick out the main points under each one and explain them in a brief paragraph.

- **Warnings:** Some students see the word summarize and make one of two mistakes. The first mistake that some students make is coping one or more sentences from their sources that seem to describe the topic. The other common mistake is putting the information into their own words but missing important details.

- **Format:** Unless the assignment directs otherwise, a summary is written in paragraph form. If there is no length requirement given in the assignment, students can gauge the length by allowing about one paragraph for each page of information summarized.

Diagram

Assignments requesting the students to "diagram" want them to gather information and create a visual depiction of some sort. This diagram can be a chart, graph, time line, cluster map, or other visual representation of the information. Sometimes the type of visual representation may be specified or it may be left up to the student to decide what will work the best.

Example: Diagram the learning styles discussed in class to highlight their shared characteristics.

> ❧ **Key words:** The key words are "diagram," "learning styles," and "shared characteristics."

> ❧ **Description:** Successful students know they will be able to choose which type of visual depiction they will use. They also know they need to come up with a list of characteristics for each learning style and then see which learning styles share which characteristics.

> ❧ **Warnings:** Some students use the same type of visual depiction time after time. This is not the best way to display the information in all cases, however. For example, a time line would not be effective in this instance.

> ❧ **Format:** The assignment format depends on the type of visual depiction chosen, but an important thing to remember regardless of the type of depiction is it should be neat and orderly. The use of colors can help highlight certain areas of the chart, but students should be careful to not make it too busy.

Trace

Assignments requesting the students to "trace" want them to show a progression through time whether it is a process, an event, or a transformation.

Example: Trace the events leading up to the discovery of learning styles.

> ❧ **Key words:** The key words are "trace," "up to the discovery," and "learning styles."

> ❧ **Description:** Successful students know they need to look at what

prompted researchers to look into the possibility of learning styles and what they did to pinpoint the different kinds of learning styles.

Warnings: Students who do not read the prompt carefully may not trace the right set of events.

Format: Unless specified, there are several different ways to present this information. Students could use a time line. Other possible formats are lists, steps, and paragraphs.

Outline

Assignments requesting the students to "outline" are instructing them to pick out the main points or key events. These assignments work well to show basic understanding of a complex theory or concept. They also work well when students need to demonstrate understanding and comprehension of reading assignments.

Example: Outline the characteristics and pros and cons of one learning style.

Key words: The key words are "outline," "characteristics and pros and cons," and "learning style."

Description: Successful students know they have to create a three-part outline for this assignment using the three main points listed in the prompt, each with its own main points and details. They also know they have to plan an organizational method that shows fairly equal levels of detail for each main point.

Warnings: Students who struggle with outlining make one of two mistakes. The first mistake is not using an organizational method. Students fail to plan out how deeply they will go into the outline and are unable to keep their organization consistent. The second mistake is giving too much detail. This type of assignment should contain the main points and essential details, but minor details should be left out of the final project.

 Format: This project should be presented in an outline format.

Identify

Assignments requesting the students to "identify" are asking them to name something specific. These prompts may clarify how many items need to be identified or in what manner they should be presented.

Example: Identify in a short paragraph five methods students can use to develop their verbal learning skills.

 Key words: The key words are "identify," "paragraph," "five," and "verbal learning skills."

 Description: Successful students know they will need to find or recall information on verbal learning skills and write a paragraph about how students can help develop their skills. They do not need to include their opinions or justifications, but simply list the items asked for.

 Warnings: Some students may take the time to evaluate the merit of each of these methods, but this is not what the question is asking. Another error is not clearly reading the prompt that tells them to write the answer in paragraph form.

 Format: While this prompt asks for a paragraph, some identify assignments do not specify or ask for a list of items.

Comment

Assignments requesting the students to "comment" are asking them to discuss a specific portion of the topic in a clear, concise, and organized manner. The assignments assign a specific sub-topic or give a choice of sub-topics to discuss.

Example: Comment on the common struggles of visual learners in college level classes.

- **Key words:** The key words are "comment," "struggles," and "visual learners."

- **Description:** Successful students know they need to write about the problems visual learners have in class.

- **Warnings:** A careless mistake with this type of prompt occurs when students fail to limit their answers to the specifications in the prompt. In this example, a mistake is not limiting answers to struggles in class. Another common mistake is when students evaluate and judge the comments instead of making statements.

- **Format:** This prompt looks for a written answer in paragraph form. The length of the answer depends on the amount of information to be commented on. In this instance, a paragraph would suffice.

DECIPHER LEVEL TWO DIRECTIVE WORDS

Level Two directive words ask the student to take the information one step further than presenting the facts in a specific manner. These types of assignments require students to interpret information and find ways to make connections about the topic or more sub-points of the topic. Projects at this level include an equal mixture of facts and personal connections and interpretations. It is important for students to remember, however, that all connections and interpretations should be backed by credible sources.

Discuss

Assignments requesting the students to "discuss" want them to examine the topic and talk about the validity, pros and cons, or benefits and disadvantages of the topic. Discussing a topic is showing all sides of it in an impartial manner, but it takes analytical skills to be able to come up with and organize the information properly.

Example: There were three main benefits to determining learning styles presented during class lectures. Discuss these benefits.

- **Key words:** The key words are "three," "benefits," and "discuss."

- **Description:** Successful students know they need to recall the information presented in the lecture and think about the validity of each of the benefits. They state their opinions about the validity of the benefits and back them up with explanations from the lecture, other sources, and reasoning.

- **Warnings:** Discussing prompts want the students to show all side of the issues so they need to take care to not write a one-sided or weighted answer to the question.

- **Format:** The discussion may be presented in paragraph form. In this instance, there are three paragraphs, one for each of the benefits listed.

Compare

Assignments requesting the students to "compare" ask them to take two or more seemingly different topics and find and discuss similarities. In some cases the similarities are obvious and in other cases the similarities are not obvious until the student has examined and analyzed the topics.

Example: Compare the intuitive learner with the verbal learner.

- **Key words:** The key words are "compare," "intuitive learner," and "verbal learner."

- **Description:** Successful students know they need to find thorough descriptions of these two types of learners and think about the characteristics for each one. They then need to draw conclusions about these characteristics to see where the similarities lie.

- **Warnings:** Some students are easily frustrated when the similarities are not readily apparent. They fail to think critically and give up without giving the assignment a chance.

- **Format:** The most common way to present this information is in paragraph form, but some students may prefer to use a Venn diagram to highlight the similarities.

Contrast

Assignments requesting the students to "contrast" ask them to take two seemingly similar topics and highlight the differences. Similar to the compare prompts, the differences can be fairly obvious or they may not be apparent without a thorough examination.

Example: Contrast sensing learners with sequential learners.

- **Key words:** The key words are "contrast," "sensing learners," and "sequential learners."

- **Description:** Successful students know they need to look at the learning styles that have similarities and think about what makes each one unique. Their finished assignment will show how, though the learning styles are similar, they have unique features.

- **Warnings:** Similar to the compare prompts, some students get frustrated when the requested information is not readily recognizable.

- **Format:** Contrast prompts result in the answers being written in paragraph form, but they can also be presented in a Venn diagram or a cluster map.

Illustrate

Assignments requesting the students to "illustrate" are asking them to take a topic and come up with examples that help show the audience the meaning of the topic. These examples can be found in lecture notes, texts, and other resources, but students who apply the topic or concept to their lives will be able to come up with unique illustrations.

Example: Illustrate the ways active learners and reflective learners can help each other.

- **Key words:** The key words are "illustrate," "active," "reflective," and "help."

- **Description:** Successful students know they need to look at the deficiencies of each of these types of learners and see if the advantages of the other type can fill the void in some way. They then need to connect these relationships with specific examples.

- **Warnings:** Some students stop at the point where they have made the relationships. While this is an important step, they need to go one step further to illustrate what they are saying with the connections and examples.

 Format: There are several ways students can present this information. They can write the information in paragraph or essay form or they could list each way and write out the example underneath it.

Apply

Assignments requesting the students to "apply" want them to take a concept or idea and show how it can work in different settings and situations. This type of project requires thorough understanding of the topic or concept to be able to show how it will function or react in a different or real-life setting.

Example: Apply the steps for determining a learning style preference to yourself.

 Key words: The key words are "apply," "steps," "learning style," and "self."

 Description: Successful students know they need to take themselves through the steps to determine their individual learning style preferences. They explain how they worked through the steps and make a conclusion as to their learning style preference.

 Warnings: Some students may not actually apply the steps to their lives and instead go right to the conclusion. While the conclusion is important, the professor uses this prompt to see that the students understood the steps in the process not just the end result.

 Format: The final project is an essay that explains how the process applied to the student's situation and also highlights the results.

Cause

Assignments requesting the students to discuss the "cause" of a topic are asking students to explain the event or events that lead up to another event. They need to be able to look at information and figure out which events are relevant to the topic and which may be concurrent but are not directly related.

Example: Sara is a physical learner who is struggling in her study skills lecture. What are some possible causes for her struggles?

- **Key words:** The key words are "physical learner," "lecture," and "possible causes."

- **Description:** Successful students know they have to predict possible causes based on the information they know about physical learners and the reported struggles they have in lectures. The answer to this question is not found in the lecture notes or in the textbook, but the information leading to the answers will be.

- **Warnings:** Some students may list the struggles that physical learners have, but if they fail to use the information to answer the question about possible causes they may lose points.

- **Format:** This type of prompt may be answered in paragraph or list form.

Effect

Assignments requesting the students to work with the "effect" of an event can ask the students either to discuss what happened in a real situation as a direct result of one event, or they may ask the students to predict what could happen in a hypothetical situation using the information they already know about the topic.

Example: Mike, a visual learner, began studying with Jane, a verbal learner. What are some possible effects of this relationship for each of them?

- **Key words:** The key words are "visual learner," "verbal learner," "effects," and "relationship."

- **Description:** Successful students know the first thing they need to do is see how the characteristics of visual learners can balance the characteristics of verbal learners and vice versa. They know they need to form their answer by showing how the relationship will affect both students.

- **Warnings:** Some students determine how verbal and visual learners can balance each other but fail to specify the effects for each person, thus not answering the prompt.

- **Format:** The information for this prompt can be presented in a list or a paragraph. In this instance, since there are two people, the effects could also be presented in a Venn diagram.

Relate

Assignments requesting the students to "relate" are asking them to show the connections between two or more people, events, or concepts. The assignment asks students to illustrate these relationships through examples and illustrations.

Example: Relate global learners to sequential learners.

- **Key words:** The key words are "relate," "global learners," and "sequential learners."

- **Description:** Successful students find quality descriptions of both types of learners and look for their similarities and differences.

They use the information to explain in what ways working together would be helpful for each of them and how they would clash when working together.

🔖 **Warnings:** Some students may write the descriptions of each type of learner and fail to make the connections on how they are related.

🔖 **Format:** These types of prompts require answers to be written in paragraph form.

Demonstrate

Assignments requesting the students to "demonstrate" are asking them to show or prove something about the topic. Students can make this proof by using a mixture of opinions and judgments with facts, figures, and citations from experts.

Example: Demonstrate how a struggling student may use learning styles to help improve their grades.

🔖 **Key words:** The key words are "demonstrate," "struggling," "learning styles," and "improve."

🔖 **Description:** Successful students know they have to look at the process of using learning styles along with the benefits of using learning styles and mesh the two to explain how struggling students can benefit. They take the information and write an essay incorporating the information with proof in the form of facts, figures, and expert opinion.

🔖 **Warnings:** Some students discuss the benefits of using learning styles and fail to apply it to struggling students along with the process. A demonstration prompt requires students to show their knowledge and prove its validity.

🐦 **Format:** This type of prompt requires answers to be written out in essay or paragraph form.

DECIPHER LEVEL THREE DIRECTIVE WORDS

Level Three directive words require the students to do the most critical thinking. These types of assignments ask the students to evaluate and apply the information. A basic format for these types of assignments requires students to make a statement and defend it with facts found through research.

Review

Assignments requesting the students to "review" want them to give a survey of the topic that praises the good points and criticizes the bad points. When students are asked to review a topic, the best thing they can do is think about a movie review and follow that format: include a quick summary, discuss the good points, discuss the bad points, and then give a judgment.

Example: Review the use of learning styles by college students.

🐦 **Key words:** The key words are "review" and "learning styles."

🐦 **Description:** Successful students know they need to give a brief overview about the theory of learning styles, list the benefits of utilizing this theory with examples, list the disadvantages of utilizing this theory with examples, and then give a judgment as to whether they think the use of learning styles theory is a good use of time for college students.

🐦 **Warnings:** The review of good points and bad points should be a personal opinion backed up with expert opinion, proven examples, and logical reasoning. It should not be copied from a source.

Format: Reviews are written in paragraph form.

Prove

Assignments requesting the students to "prove" will make a statement and then ask the students to agree or disagree with it and then prove their side of the issue.

Example: Read the following statement, decide if you agree or disagree with it and then prove your side of the issue:

"Students who lean toward a verbal learning style are more likely to succeed in college than those who lean toward other learning styles."

  Key words: The key words are "read," "decide," and "prove."

  Description: Successful students know they need to make a decision of agreement or disagreement with the statement. Before they do so, they need to review the characteristics, advantages, and disadvantages of each type of learning style. After they make their decision, they look for examples, expert opinion, facts, and figures to show their decision is the best decision.

  Warnings: A common error for students is not taking one side but instead showing the pros and cons of both sides. Another common error on this type of assignment is not giving enough solid proof of their opinion and instead restating their opinion in a variety of ways. Finally, a third common error is trying to prove their side of the issue with emotions instead of fact.

  Format: These assignments are written in essay or paragraph form.

Interpret

Assignments requesting the students to "interpret" information want them to look at information and explain its significance. Students are also expected to include their thoughts and opinions on the information and back them up with facts and logical reasoning.

Example: Interpret this study: "A recent study found that 62 percent of students who take a learning styles mini-course during their first semester of college graduate while only 47 percent of students who do not take the mini-course during their first semester of college graduate." The students are provided with the rest of the study report including the methodology.

- **Key words:** The key words are "interpret" and "study."

- **Description:** Successful students know they need to read through the entire study and break it down into a few sub-topics. Then they need to analyze the results and validity of each sub-topic. Then they draw a conclusion about the study and back it up with information, facts, and reasoning.

- **Warnings:** Some students look at the results of the study and fail to look at the methodology, process, and other information about the study to make their interpretation. Other students fail to include their opinions and instead re-state the findings with out interpretation.

- **Format:** These assignments require the answer to be written in paragraph or essay form.

Evaluate

Assignments requesting students to "evaluate" want them to comment on the value of the topic. Students are expected to explain the problem, issue, or topic, and discuss the advantages and disadvantages with a final recommendation.

Example: Evaluate the process of balancing the active and reflective learner.

> **Key words:** The key words are "evaluate," "process," and "active and reflective learner."

> **Description:** Successful students know they first have to explain the differences between active and reflective learning. Then, they point out the problems for each type of learner if they cannot find a useful balance. They show the advantage and disadvantages of trying to strike a balance. Finally, successful students make a final recommendation on whether it is useful to try to strike a balance between these two learning styles.

> **Warnings:** Some students list the characteristics and the advantages and disadvantages but they fail to take the final step of including their opinions about the value of the process.

> **Format:** These assignments are completed in paragraph or essay form.

Justify

Assignments requesting students to "justify" give them an opportunity to develop and state an opinion about a topic. Then, the students are required to justify or prove why their opinion is valid by showing examples, expert testimony, comparisons, and reasoning.

Example: Decide whether you think using the theory of learning styles is an effective method to improve grades and study habits. Justify your answer.

📚 **Key words:** The key words are "learning styles," "effective," and "justify."

📚 **Description:** Successful students first take time to develop their opinion. Then they look for three to four main points to support their opinion and make sure they have examples, expert testimony, comparisons, studies, and reasoning to back up their opinion. From there they write a project that clearly states their opinion and uses sources to justify why their opinion is the best opinion.

📚 **Warnings:** Some students fail to use enough information to justify their opinion. The best way to overcome this obstacle is to make sure they have a variety of information from several sources.

📚 **Format:** This type of assignment is presented in paragraph or essay form.

Respond

Assignments requesting students to "respond" to a topic want them to state and back up their opinions. The response may be to a concept discussed in class as a whole or the professor may present a statement relating to a concept discussed in class and ask the students to respond to it.

Example: Respond to the following statement: "The best way for students to guarantee success in college is to determine their learning style and use this knowledge to their advantage."

📚 **Key words:** The key words are "respond," "guarantee," "learning styles," and "advantage."

📚 **Description:** Successful students first spend time thinking about the statement and evaluating its validity. After they have formed an opinion about the statement, they have to find reasons to back up this opinion. These reasons can be a variety of information including expert opinion, facts, figures, logic, or comparisons.

🐚 **Warnings:** Some students fail to form a definitive opinion about the statement and tend to jump back and forth on both sides of the issue. Other students fail to back up their opinions.

🐚 **Format:** This type of assignment is presented in paragraph or essay form.

Support or Oppose

Assignments requesting students to "support or oppose" want them to show the validity or invalidity of a concept or statement. The support can come in the form of examples, expert opinion, comparisons, and logical reasoning.

Example: Support or oppose the following statement:

"Students are out of luck if they have a learning style that does not meld with a professor's teaching style."

🐚 **Key words:** The key words are "learning style," "teaching style," and "support or oppose."

🐚 **Description:** Successful students know they need to decide if they support or oppose the statement. Then they need to gather and use evidence that supports their opinion.

🐚 **Warnings:** Some students do not completely agree or disagree with the given statements so they have a difficult time working on the project. It is important to remember they do not need to agree with what they are writing as long as they present a solid support or opposition to the statement.

- **Format:** This type of assignment is presented in paragraph or essay form.

Analyze

Assignments requesting students to "analyze" want them to break down the subject into sections and go over the advantages and disadvantages of each section. The project should contain a conclusion about the topic after each section is thoroughly reviewed.

Example: Analyze the different learning styles.

- **Key words:** The key words are "analyze" and "learning styles."

- **Description:** Successful students know each learning style has to be treated as a sub-topic. They have to determine the pros and cons for each learning style, describe them in the assignment, and make a final conclusion about the learning styles. This conclusion could be about learning styles as a whole, the individual learning styles, or both.

- **Warnings:** Some students list the pros and cons of the learning styles and fail to use the information to draw a conclusion. This can result in a major loss of points since the conclusion is the part of the assignment that shows the professor what the students think about the learning styles.

- **Format:** This type of assignment is presented in paragraph or essay form.

Argue

Assignments requesting students to "argue" want them to take a side on the issue, concept, or provided statement and prove why one side is more correct or more advantageous than the other side of the issue.

Example: Argue for or against the use of the theory of learning styles by college students.

- **Key words:** The key words are "argue" and "learning styles."

- **Description:** Successful students first have to decide if they think it is advantageous for students to use the theory of learning styles or not. Then, they have to determine the reasons for their opinion and gather information such as expert opinion, facts, figures, comparisons, and examples to help illustrate why their opinion is correct.

- **Warnings:** One of the biggest problems with arguing is some students fail to choose a side and jump back and forth listing the pros and cons of both sides of the issue without forming any sort of connection or conclusion.

- **Format:** This type of assignment is presented in paragraph or essay form.

Criticize

Assignments requesting students to "criticize" want them to make a judgment on the merit or correctness of a topic, concept, or statement. The students are expected to analyze the topic by discussing the advantages and disadvantages and using the discussions to come to a conclusion about the merit of the topic.

Example: Criticize the learning style theory.

- **Key words:** The key words are "criticize" and "learning style theory."

- **Description:** Successful students know they need to decide whether the learning style theory is valuable to college students. After they decide on the merit of the theory, they show how its advantages and disadvantages support their opinion. Again, they do this through the use of expert opinion, facts, figures, comparisons, and logical reasoning.

Warnings: Some students do a nice job of listing the advantages and disadvantages and implying a side on the issue, but they fail to connect all the information together in a critical conclusion that shows their view of and answer to the prompt.

Format: This type of assignment is presented in paragraph or essay form.

HANDLE HYBRID DIRECTIVES

The previous examples show students how to approach assignment prompts that ask them to use one directive. There will be times, however, when assignment prompts will include two or more directives. The best way for students to handle these prompts is to progress through the directives starting with the level one directives, then completing level two directives, and finally finishing up with the level three directives.

Here are some examples:

List and evaluate the different learning styles. The successful student first lists the learning styles and then moves on to evaluate each one according to the information on how to evaluate a topic.

Explain and review the process of determining a learning style preference. The successful student first lists the steps in the process and then goes back and fills in the review of each step.

🖋 **Identify three disadvantages for and explain the effects of aural learning preferences.** The successful student first determines the disadvantages and then moves on to determine the effects of each disadvantage.

It is important for students to remember they cover all of the directives when completing the assignment so they do not lose points for the careless mistake of not following directions.

CASE STUDY: DAWN ROHM

Dawn Rohm is an instructor and systems administrator at St. Norbert College in De Pere, Wisconsin. She earned her bachelor's in mathematics in 1997 from St. Norbert College, her master's in computer science in 2000 from the University of Wisconsin Milwaukee and is expecting her Ph.D. in engineering in 2009 from the University of Wisconsin Milwaukee.

Dawn's thoughts on student adjustment:

First semester freshmen struggle with the ability to take responsibility for learning the material themselves. While we provide them with the tools to learn (lectures, labs, assignments, etc), they fail to take advantage of those tools. I have found that freshman often don't feel the need to do ungraded assignments. If there is no immediate accountability, they just don't do it. Freshmen also tend to struggle with large assignments. They need to set small deadlines to ensure they are able to complete the assignment.

Dawn's thoughts on student distractions and advice:

Working too much can harm a student's studies — whenever possible they should try to avoid working more than 20 hours per week. The need to set up a whole new network of friends on arrival at college takes time for some. Forcing themselves to study between classes can give them time to socialize in the evenings.

Dawn's thoughts on important study tips:

The night before the exam is NOT the time to realize you don't know the material. If they keep up with their studies, the night before the exam shouldn't require much extra effort! They need to maintain a list of things that need to be done somewhere (on paper or electronically) and be aware of their deadlines.

SPECIAL CONSIDERATIONS FOR ASSIGNMENTS

There are four basic types of assignments found in college courses. While they all have similarities, each has its own special considerations. Students who understand the idiosyncrasies of each type of assignment have a better chance of success than those who do not understand the format of the assignment they undertake.

RESEARCH THE RESEARCH PAPER

Simply defined, a research paper is a paper that uses information from other sources to solve a problem. The degree of difficulty of a research paper varies depending on which level of directives the paper uses. Most research papers result from prompts containing level one directives because these directives require research-heavy papers. They contain few, if any, personal thoughts and opinions.

Paper prompts from level two directives can be research papers as well, because while level two directives require more thought and analysis than level one, they might not require the statement of opinions.

Research papers rarely result from level three directives because these directives require the students to form and support opinions. Research papers should be impartial accounts of the information.

There are several characteristics of effective research papers:

- **They contain researched, sourced, and cited material.** Failing to cite sources is considered plagiarism and can result in academic repercussions from the student's institution and could go as far as legal action.

- **They are well-written.** This means they contain proper language, correct grammar and mechanics, and flow well. They are also easy to read and understand without being too simplistic.

- **They are well-organized.** They contain an introduction, a body, a conclusion, and a works cited page or bibliography.

Analyzing the Analysis Paper

Analysis papers are similar to research papers, but they contain more of the student's personal thoughts and opinions than research papers. Analysis papers result from level three directives and are one-sided accounts that state the topic, explain a position on that topic, present points with support that prove the position to be correct or advantageous, and conclude with a final recommendation and reiteration of the writer's original opinion.

While analysis papers do not rely on it, students may use research to help prove their opinion about the topic. The research may be more one-sided than that found in a research paper. There will be instances when the student will not need to research for an analysis paper. These instances include analyses of studies where the proof will consist of reasoning and examples from the study; analyses of literary works where the proof will consist of reasoning and examples from the work; and analyses of events where the proof will consist of reasoning and examples from the event.

PRESENTING THE PRESENTATION

A presentation is indirectly based on a research paper or an analysis paper. Even when the student is not directed to write the paper as a specific part of the assignment, the "paper" is the written form of the presentation. Any level of directive can prompt presentations. Regardless of the type of directive, there are important steps successful students take to promote success with the presentation:

- **Successful students** write a script for every presentation even if they only use note cards during the actual presentation.

- **Successful students** prepare by reading and practicing their scripts and then moving to an outline. Through practice, students can recite their presentation using note cards containing a simple outline or key words.

- **Successful students** know presentations need an introduction, a body, and a conclusion.

- **Successful students** create handouts and visual aids that enhance their material. These can be visual depictions of the material such as time lines, charts, graphs, or maps.

ALLOW ENOUGH TIME

There are occasions when professors announce or hand out the information for an assignment with little time to spare before the due date. This is rare. It is tempting for students to wait to look at the assignment sheet when they have two or three weeks until the due date. This can be detrimental to students who underestimate the time it will take to complete an assignment or who run into unexpected snags along the way.

START EARLY

Successful students start early on their assignments. This does not mean they are working on assignments weeks or months in advance, but they start on it in case things take longer than anticipated. If they have a clear understanding of what is expected of them for the assignment, they can spend time thinking and brainstorming before they have to sit down and get to work.

The first thing they do is read through the assignment description. During this read through, they take preliminary notes and jot down any questions they may have about the assignment, the topic, or the format so that as soon as they have an opportunity to discuss the assignment with their professor they have their questions ready.

At this point, successful students:

- Pay attention to the details, such as the length, format, and any additional materials that need to be developed.

- Determine which citation format they will be expected to use and find the necessary information if they are not familiar with the format.

- Figure out the types of sources they are required to use and determine whether their resources will be readily available.

- Set arbitrary deadlines so they can work ahead and avoid the stress of the night-before-its-due cramming session.

- Make a plan to allow at least three days for the physical writing process for a paper or practicing for a presentation.

- Write their deadlines and plan into their schedule.

- Appreciate the value of thinking. Students who start early can spend a few days or weeks thinking about and analyzing the topic to help them come up more ideas.

Choose a Prompt

An assignment sheet may give the students a choice in prompts. This is an opportunity for students because they have the chance to personalize the assignment as much as possible, and if they start early enough they can think about their choices to pick one that interests them. Students may have a difficult time choosing a prompt. Here are some hints to help facilitate that decision:

- Students should first mark which prompt or prompts pop out to them as interesting. If nothing pops out as interesting, students should look at it from the other perspective and cross off the prompts they are not interested in using. Either way, they have narrowed the choices.

🐚 Students who have a difficult time choosing may come up with a topic sentence for each remaining prompt and then weigh the pros and cons of each one.

🐚 Students who continue to have difficulty can take the topic sentences to the professor and ask for advice or thoughts on their work so far to help them eliminate more options.

CHOOSE A TOPIC

The topic for an assignment may be specified by the prompt. Other times, the prompt leaves the specific topic up to the student. Choosing a topic can be overwhelming and difficult, but here are some hints that successful students use when they are stumped about a topic:

🐚 They look for a topic that interests them or for something they want to explore further.

🐚 They take a short list of possible topics to the professor and seek advice.

🐚 They find a fresh, new, or interesting topic and work it to fit in to the assignment parameters.

🐚 They go to the textbook and look at the case studies, asides, and examples to see if anything sparks their interest.

🐚 They brainstorm.

They freewrite. To freewrite, the student writes the general topic at the top of a sheet of paper. The student then sets a timer for a specific time, perhaps five or ten minutes. Then the student writes whatever comes to mind. If they cannot think of anything to write, they write: "I cannot think of anything to write" until something else pops into their head. At the end of the session, the student reads through the paper to see if any good topics appeared.

 They apply the general topic to their life to see if there is any specific topic that relates.

RESEARCH EARLY & EAGERLY

Not all assignments require research, but those that do are best started early. The first step in researching for an assignment is determining if it requires research. In most cases, however, the opposite causes problems. Students assume the assignment will not require research and then find themselves in a bind the night before the due date trying to find appropriate sources. There are ways to avoid this frenzy— by having a solid research strategy in place and ready to go for any assignment that comes along.

AVOID CRAMMING IN RESEARCH

Students who wait until the last minute to do their research run into a variety of problems. If the professor has given the same assignment to at least one whole section. If the assignment gives a specific topic, there will be many students trying to get the same information. Successful students avoid this rush by going to the library before other students have taken a second look at the assignment sheet.

Another problem for students cramming research in at the end is there will be times when the perfect resource is at a different library and students have to wait for it to come through an intralibrary loan. Depending on the library system and where the book is located, it can take anywhere from a few days to a week or two to access that resource.

Finally, few professors have sympathy for students who are unable to obtain the necessary materials to complete their assignment because they waited too long to start researching. It is a shame to miss out on a successful grade due to wasted time.

Find Credible and Current Sources

It is common for students to visit the Internet, use Google to find their assignment topic, print off a few pages, and call it a day when it comes to research. This may be okay in high school, but it is not a good way to research in college. One of the best ways to increase chances of success is for students to make a special effort to find credible and current sources for their assignments. There are a variety of ways to do this:

- **Successful students** start with general resources such as biographical encyclopedias, general encyclopedias, dictionaries, and textbooks to give them an overview of their topic. These sources may not be the best sources to cite in the assignment, but they can be a fantastic basis to give ideas for further research.

- **Successful students** take the time to get a tour of the library. This gives them information about the university's online resources as well as the library's special stacks, collections, and policies. All of this information makes researching easier.

- **Successful students** know most professors will not accept Web sites as resources unless they are sources of credible information.

- **Successful students** look for a variety of information including journal articles, personal accounts, and books.

> Successful students take their topic, thesis, and found resources to the professor and ask if he or she can suggest any other resources for them to use.

KNOW WHEN TO STOP

It could be possible to continue researching forever. Successful students know at some point they need to stop and move on to other parts of the assignment. The key is to stop at the right moment. This is imperative because once the student is in the writing mode of the assignment, he or she will not want to stop and go back to do more research. If there is not time to go back and gather more research, the lack of information can result in weak arguments in the finished project.

Here are some tips from successful students who know when to stop:

> All main points of the final project should have two to three resources.

> Students need to try to get at least two different types of sources before they quit researching.

> It is important to continue researching until all of the student's questions about the topic are answered.

> Finally, students make copies or printouts of their resources when they find them so they do not have to go back and search for the original if they missed something along the way.

CRAFT THE SEARCH TERMS

Students may have difficulty finding information for their topic and find themselves going around in circles finding the same sources over and over again. It is frustrating for students when this happens. There are ways to prevent this frustration by carefully crafting search terms:

- Successful students create a research log to help them remember which search terms they use. This can be as simple as a list on a piece of paper to as advanced as a chart that shows which search terms were used in which databases.

- Successful students also break down their topics to find more specific information. Instead of searching for "study skills" and hoping to find specific information on each of their main points, they search using keywords related to each of their main points.

- Successful students learn how to conduct electronic searches using Booleans, wild cards, and limiters.

- Some successful students keep a written log such as the one following to help them remember what, when, and where they have searched for information. Then whenever they use a search term, they record the information. This is also a source for them to keep track of possible additional search terms as they think of them.

KEYWORD	DATE	PLACES USED (DATABASES, SEARCH ENGINES)	SOURCES FOUND

WRITING IS ONLY A SMALL PORTION OF SUCCESS

One of the biggest mistakes students make when completing writing assignments is failing to recognize the actual writing of the assignment is just a small percentage of the work necessary for success. Successful students go through a number of steps and consider their options while completing their assignments. It may sound tedious or overwhelming at first, but successful students realize these steps and considerations soon become second nature to them and eventually writing assignments become easier.

THINK ABOUT TOPICS IN RELATION TO ASSIGNMENTS

Successful students have realized that writing assignments rarely require them to simply write down all of the information they know about a topic. When they are given a specific question to answer or writing prompt to follow, they need to carefully read the assignment, consider the directive words (see Chapter 17), and make a plan to apply the information they have found about the topic in a way that answers the question or prompt presented to them.

Example: Compare the steps in the writing process presented by the author to the writing process you currently use.

- A successful student would know they need to look at the similarities and differences between their writing process and the author's writing process rather than simply describing everything about the writing process.

- Writing assignments may be less specific and give a general topic or a type of paper and allow the students the freedom to narrow their topics from there. Especially in these cases, successful students know they need to examine their topic and make sure it fits in the realm of the given assignment.

THESIS IS A BASIS

The thesis is the most important sentence in any assignment. Thesis statements are not just for papers. They can be an extremely useful starting point for any assignment because they help students focus their ideas and decide how to proceed. Furthermore, theses act as a road map to help students stay focused as they proceed through the assignment.

When writing their thesis statements, successful students remember the statements need to be:

- **Concise.** Successful students know the thesis should define information that they can present in the length of the assignment. For example, a thesis that requires the reader to describe World War II is not concise enough for a five-page paper. Instead, the student would have to narrow the thesis to a specific battle, describing a specific cause, the reasons why a specific country joined the war, or the effects of the war on women in a certain part of the country.

- **General.** Successful students know the thesis should allow for enough information to fill the minimum length requirements without redundancy. For example, a thesis about describing three places to research in the library will not provide enough information to fill a five-page paper, but it may be enough for a one-page paper.

- **Interesting and arguable.** This is especially true in instances when students have complete freedom over their topics. For example, a thesis about stating the differences between apples and oranges is not going to be interesting because most people already know the differences between apples and oranges. It also is not arguable because most people agree that apples and oranges are different. A thesis that promises to describe the similarities between apples and oranges, on the other hand, is interesting and arguable since most people will agree that the similarities are not easily seen.

- **Appropriate.** If the thesis does not follow the assignment requirements, the final paper will not follow the assignment requirements either. Successful students verify that the thesis follows the assignment by turning the assignment prompt into a question and making sure the thesis answers the question.

- **Short.** Successful students try to keep their thesis statements at ten words or less. This helps them think in-depth about what they want to say and what they want to cover in their paper. While it may seem tedious to do this, it is an important planning step that will pay off later in the assignment process.

WRITING PROCESS

The writing process should be used regardless of the type of assignment because it can easily apply to papers, speeches, presentations, and projects. Successful students follow this writing process for all of their assignments:

1. **Think about the assignment.** Successful students read through the assignment description and start thinking about the requirements and topics before they do any physical work on the assignment. This part of the process allows them to think about possible topics and what angle they want to cover on the topic.

2. **Brainstorm and write a working outline.** During this step, successful students write down all of the information they can think of about the topic as well as questions they have that will require research. After they have brainstormed, they take the information and organize it into several main points. This is a working outline, and it may be changed throughout the process. It primarily serves as a way to get started.

BRAINSTORMING TECHNIQUES	
Freewriting	Freewriting is a technique where the brainstormer spends a set amount of time writing about the topic. When freewriting, it is important to just write and not worry about sentences, complete thoughts, grammar, spelling, or other mechanics. The important thing is to simply write whatever comes to mind regardless if it is on topic or not. If nothing comes to mind, write "I can't think of anything to write" until something else comes to mind. After the time limit, students go back and read through the writing and highlight any relevant ideas.
Listing	Listing is a brainstorming technique where the brainstormer simply lists everything he or she can think of about the topic. This can be one large list or it can be broken down into sub-topics.
Visual Depictions	Visual depictions have the brainstormer creating maps, webs, or clusters of the information about the topic. This technique starts with the topic in the middle and the information around the outside. Brainstormers can use lines and circles to connect related ideas to create the clusters.

BRAINSTORMING TECHNIQUES	
Cubing	Cubing is a brainstorming technique that requires the brainstormer to do six specific tasks with the topic: describe it, compare/contrast it, associate it, analyze it, apply it, and argue for or against it.
Reporting	Reporting has the brainstormer act as a reporter and look for answers to the six journalistic questions: Who? What? When? Where? Why? and How? Students who use this technique can get a good sense of what areas of the topic they need to research and what areas they are more familiar with.
Use Resources	When all other methods of brainstorming fail, students turn to the reference section at the library. The dictionaries, thesaurus, and encyclopedias are great starting points to help get the ideas flowing.

3. **Write the thesis.** At this point students have spent time thinking and writing about the topic. Now is the time to narrow the information to one concise, arguable, and interesting thesis statement. After writing the thesis statement, the students need to go back to the working outline to see if any of the main points need to be changed, moved, or deleted.

4. **Research.** Students now spend time researching the topic. Because the thesis statement sets the paper up to be interesting and arguable, the researching stage is important for the student to find information about each of the main points to explain them – there should be two to three resources for each main point. If this is an assignment that does not require research, the student will then spend this time brainstorming specific ideas and information for each main point.

5. **Write a detailed outline.** This is the stage where students read through their research, take notes, and plug the information into the working outline. It will likely involve going back and forth from notes, research materials, and the outline, but spending

time on this to get a nice, solid outline will help in the next step.

6. **Write.** A problem for many students is becoming distracted while writing their rough draft. The most important thing to remember is that this is a rough draft and the main idea of this step is to get the ideas on paper in a relatively organized and comprehensible manner. Successful students have found some ways to help them do this:

> ☙ Use only the outline to aid in writing to keep the focus on the writing and not additional research.

> ☙ Plan time to write the entire paper in one sitting.

> ☙ Find a quiet place with no Internet or other distractions.

7. **Put it away.** Successful students find that they can get frazzled while working on an assignment constantly. It can be helpful to write the first draft and then put it away. Of course this does require planning so that they have time to do this before the assignment deadline, but most successful students will tell you it is worth it in the end because it gives them a fresh look at the assignment when they go back to finalize everything.

8. **Finalize the assignment.** After the assignment has "rested" for a few days, students can revise it. This involves looking for grammatical errors and typos as well as the cohesiveness of ideas. This is also a time to eliminate wordiness and redundancy to make the assignment as concise as possible.

At this point it is important to double-check the conclusion. Students may tend to skimp on the conclusion because they are tired of the assignment by the time they get to the end or they rush to get it done. When the assignment is finalized, students need to think about presenting the assignment to the professor:

- ❧ Double-check hard copies of papers to ensure the printing is readable and contains all of the pages.

- ❧ Clearly label papers that will be turned in electronically.

- ❧ Practice speeches and presentations. Use visual aids during rehearsal if applicable.

- ❧ Prepare and double-check audience handouts for accuracy and proper grammar. Make sure there are enough copies for the audience.

- ❧ Double-check all projects that contain multiple mediums to make sure everything is in its proper place.

OTHER CONSIDERATIONS FOR PROJECTS, PAPERS, AND PRESENTATION

Successful students also think about other considerations when completing assignments. Professors will notice the little things that make one student's assignment stand out from the rest. Students who follow these tips can help ensure their assignments will stand out for the better:

- ❧ **Know the Audience.** At times the intended audience will be specified in the assignment prompt. When there is no specified audience, the student should complete the assignment for the class instead of the professor so they do not leave out important details. For example, if the students in a Child Development class are asked to make presentations about a birth defect, they should give information that will be beneficial to the students in the audience and not the professor, who arguably already knows much of the information. Even though the professor will be grading the assignment, in most cases it is best to assume the audience is the class who has knowledge of the topic but who may need background in certain areas.

- **Cite Sources.** When in doubt, it is better to cite than to not cite and end up plagiarizing something. Colleges and universities also use plagiarism detection programs that help professors detect blatant copying of information. Students who are not sure about how to cite their sources should consult with their professor on the preferred citation method for the assignment.

- **Use proper grammar.** The lingo used in e-mail and text messaging is not appropriate for college-level assignments.

- **Make a good impression.** Rumpled, folded, or messily printed papers do not make a good impression. All assignments should look professional and neat to show that the student cares about the assignment and the class.

CASE STUDY: SARAH E. RYAN

Sarah E. Ryan is a professor in the School of Public Affairs at Baruch College, City University of New York. She is the former Director of the Bronx Defenders Debate Initiative and holds a Ph.D. in Rhetorical Criticism from the Scripps College of Communication at Ohio University. She is the author of numerous journal articles and *Think College Now*, a college-prep curriculum for 9th graders used in more than a dozen New York City schools.

Sara's thoughts on student adjustment:

Students report to the hardest adjustment is in managing the sheer volume of work. Time management is key. When students figure out how to schedule time for reading, writing, thinking, attending class, and everything else they'd like to do in college, they're well on their way to success.

CASE STUDY: SARAH E. RYAN

Sara's thoughts on student surprises:

The biggest surprise for students in academia is how much intellectual terrain exists. Their professors wrote dissertations about strange, profound things that the average human being has not heard of. Going to college opens students' eyes to the millions of intellectual projects that have been undertaken — and the horizons unexplored.

College writing is difficult for students because there are disparate expectations for student writing. English professors expect different sorts of essays than botany professors and students have different style of writing — complete with different sorts of "proof," argumentation, citation, etc. That student will become a jack-of-all-trades based upon his or her reading of each discipline, course, professor, and assignment. Of course, the key is to look for context clues — every syllabus, reading, sample paper, lecture, etc. reveals what the professor believes is solid writing and argumentation. Students must act like detectives, piecing together the clues to discern what sort of writing is considered exemplary in each circumstance.

Sara's thoughts on student distractions:

Students get worn down by the final third of a semester or quarter. Most professors assign more material than even the best students can process in the span of 10 or 15 weeks. Students who understand this and take advantage of the excitement and energy they have in the first third of the semester or quarter are the most successful. If professors offer a choice of assignments – choose the ones offered early in the semester when you are fresh! Get ahead on the readings when you can. Take care of other business like your tuition bill, FAFSA re-application early in the semester or quarter. Take advantage of that extra "push" you have early on each term.

Sara's thoughts on important study tips:

Students should figure out how really study best and commit to remember terms unless I made note cards – period. So, each semester I bought a big stack o note cards and started writing out terms the first day of class. I could watch Thursday night TV, for instance, but only if I made note cards while I watched.

Sara's thoughts on memories:

The funniest thing you'll see in New York City — with more than half-a-million college students — is the lengths students will go to study. You'll see a student crushed in

CASE STUDY: SARAH E. RYAN

between half-a-dozen people on the R train clutching a chemistry book in one hand and trying to make notes with the other hand (which is crushed between a couple of people). If you can study on the R train, you can study anywhere!

Part 5

HANDLING SPECIAL CIRCUMSTANCES

Colleges and universities try to keep up with innovations to allow more students to attend classes and to provide students with the skills they will need to be competitive in the demanding world after graduation.

UNDERSTANDING ONLINE & BLENDED CLASSES

One of the newest trends in college education is the growing need to successfully use technology. This has led to the offering of online and blended classes. Online and blended classes are perfect for people who cannot take traditional classes due to location or time constraints. Online and blended classes require extra initiative from the students to be willing to learn independently. Blended classes often have a percentage of classes in person and the rest online.

- **Participation is key.** It is not enough to log in and read what is on the board for the class. The professor needs to "see" your presence in the class in the form of participation in the online discussions.

- **Know the system.** Successful students to get to know the system and how it works, including where to find assignments, how to contact the professor directly, how to post messages, and where to post assignments.

- **Be willing to get technical help.** There will be times when the system is not working. Successful students get technical help to continue regular participation in the class.

Realize professors and classmates are real people too. Successful students are respectful of ideas, questions, and comments posted by others.

Do not underestimate the need to study. Online classes require students to study at least as much as traditional classes.

Log in to the class every day. This is the best way to find updates from the professors and successfully partake in the discussion.

Use proper online etiquette.

ONLINE ETIQUETTE RULES	
RULE	**EXAMPLE**
Be neat and professional.	It is easy to be informal and sloppy when it comes to sending e-mails. There are so many abbreviations common to e-mail and text messaging that it is easy to use them when responding to an online course, but this is the one way professors and fellow classmates can form an impression about each another so it is important to keep the format formal.
Be concise.	Everyone is busy and can get frustrated reading through redundant, repetitive messages. Keep everything to the point.
Stay on topic.	People like to be able to go back into the archives and quickly find a message. One way to facilitate this is to only address one topic per message.
Use an accurate "subject."	Again, so people can go back and easily find the message, keep the subject line accurate to the information in the message.
Be aware of typographical cues.	Using all caps is considered shouting and rude. It is also more difficult to read
Avoid inappropriate postings.	Students should make class-appropriate postings to an online or blended class. This is not the right venue for sharing chain letters or junk mail.

ONLINE ETIQUETTE RULES	
RULE	**EXAMPLE**
Clarify responses.	When responding to someone else's message, copy and paste the relevant section of the original message so readers can put the comments into perspective.
Respect others.	It is easy to say things online that would not be said face to face. Before hitting the send button, students should reread the message and make sure it is appropriate. A good rule is that if they would not say it face to face they should not say it on e-mail.
Avoid humor and sarcasm.	These rarely come through in e-mail because of the inability to convey tone of voice and facial expressions.

Professors on traditional "live" classes may also want to use online classroom technology to facilitate class projects or discussions to supplement the classroom work. The same tips apply even though it may be just a small percentage of the complete workload for the class.

MASTER GROUP PROJECTS

A growing trend in college-level classes is the dreaded group project. Most students dislike the mere thought of group projects because of all of the logistics that go into making it a success. The actual process of a group project is an important learning tool in and of itself — exactly why professors are using this method more in classes. It is rare for people to work completely independently in the real world. Group projects at the college level, even though possibly stressful, are ways to practice these necessary skills. Successful students would agree they would rather make their teamwork mistakes at the college level than when it could mean being fired or passed up for a promotion in the real world.

CHOOSE THE TEAM

There will be instances when the professor assigns groups for a project, but students are typically free to choose their teammates. Successful students try to choose students who:

- Attend class every day.
- Participate in class.

- Seem to get along with the professor.

- Are friendly.

- Care about school.

- Live on or near campus.

- Have similar studying habits as themselves.

- Have similar interests as themselves.

Students will get to know others who are studying in the same majors and minors. This will help them determine which people may be a good fit for a group project.

Take the First Step

A group project requires that students communicate with each other. Successful students know they need to set up an initial meeting as soon as possible so they can get started. When setting up the initial meeting it is important to remember the following:

- Choose a time when everyone can meet.

- Delegate one person to make sure the space is available.

- Exchange contact information, including e-mail and phone numbers.

- Make sure everyone knows where to meet.

Be the Leader

Successful students know all groups need a leader. When no one else takes the initiative to be the leader, successful students take on the role. This has advantages:

- ☙ They can direct the project the way they see fit.

- ☙ They can make sure everyone is doing their assigned parts.

- ☙ They can keep track of progress without stepping on other members' toes.

- ☙ They can work to keep the group meetings moving to not waste anyone's time.

It is important for group leaders to not become overbearing. Successful students know it is time to take a step back and examine the teamwork when:

- ☙ The majority of the group disagrees with how the leader is running the project.

- ☙ Group members make changes without consulting the rest of the group.

- ☙ There seems to be dissent among the group.

- ☙ Group members constantly disagree with the leader.

DELEGATE TASKS

The best way to delegate tasks within a group is to first find out the types of work everyone prefers doing. Successful students know it is counter-productive to ask students who prefer one type of work to do another type of work; the result is a group of people struggling to complete tasks they do not enjoy. Some students may be excellent at digging up obscure information while others are good at interviewing people.

When delegating tasks in group projects, successful students:

- Make a list of everything that needs to be done and check it against the assignment requirements to ensure they cover everything.

- Ask group members to choose the tasks they are most comfortable doing.

- Ensure the tasks are delegated equally throughout the group.

- Invite the more shy or quiet members to share their thoughts throughout the process.

Stay on Task during Group Meetings

All groups are likely to get off-task at times, but it is especially likely to happen when two or more of the group members are friends outside the group. They will start talking and before the group knows it, they have wasted time getting nothing accomplished. Other students like to complain so they will try to make the group work session into a grievance group.

Getting off task can be frustrating for students who have other work to complete or who have other commitments after the group meeting. A few students wasting time can cause unnecessary conflict in the group. Successful students have a few statements they use to get the group on task:

- "I have to meet another group in 30 minutes and I'd like to finish up so that I don't leave you with more work to do."

- "You know, it's not fair to talk about someone who isn't here."

- "I know that you guys want to make plans for this weekend, but we have to get this done tonight because I'm not going to be able to meet with you this weekend."

📖 "Let's talk about what is done compared to what we need to finish."

SET DEADLINES

Group projects may require multi-step processes that require some things to be completed before the group can move on to other parts of the assignment. Because of this the group needs to set specific deadlines and hold the members responsible for meeting them. Simply saying "We need to get A, B, and C done before we can do D, E, and F" is not enough to make sure everyone has time to get their work done. Consider the following when setting deadlines for tasks:

📖 If one of the group members cannot meet the first deadline because of the workload from other classes, assign that group member tasks from the second deadline instead.

📖 Make the deadlines reasonable by allowing enough time to make revisions but without requiring group members to drop everything else to complete this project.

📖 Whenever possible, set deadlines so the group members can complete the work at an even pace throughout the project. This will prevent the need for cramming it in right before the deadline.

RESOLVE CONFLICT

The success of the group depends on how they handle inevitable instances of conflict and disagreement. Conflict can arise for a variety of reasons — from not agreeing on how to proceed with the project to disagreeing on the details to include. Other disagreements arise when it seems one or more students are not pulling their weight. Successful students find ways to handle the conflict before there is a total breakdown in the group.

- **Be patient.** Students may need a little extra time to think things through or get their thoughts in order before they can be productive members of a group.

- **Be respectful.** It is important to remember that every member of the group is busy and there may be extenuating circumstances that cause them to not work up to the expectations that other group members have set.

- **Be flexible.** Successful students know group members may have an unexpected conflict that causes them to need help getting their part done. A way to handle this is to be flexible in the deadlines or in the delegation of tasks.

- **Make a compromise.** The best way to resolve a conflict may be to make a compromise so that everyone gets a little bit of what they want. It is better to do this than foster unrest in the group to the point of not being able to successfully complete the assignment.

- **Let it go.** There will be times that successful students need to just suck it up and do it someone else's way. One way is not always better than another, but simply different.

- **Agree to disagree.** A disagreement about how to handle situations can seem to continue with no end in sight. This is an unproductive waste of time for the group. If it is possible to move on without coming to an agreement, disagree on the topic.

- **Consult the professor.** In cases where it seems impossible to resolve a conflict, such as a group member consistently not showing up for meetings or consistently doing sub-par work, it may be necessary to discuss the issues with the professor. This should not be a meeting where the grieving group members complain constantly about the slacking student. Instead, the group members should set up an appointment and outline what has happened and ask for advice on how to handle the situation. It will be most productive to have evidence and to be non-accusatory during this meeting.

☙ **Give accurate evaluations.** In some assignments the group members will be asked to evaluate the others in the group. It is important to give accurate statements about each student so the professor can get a clear sense of how well the group worked together.

PICK UP THE SLACK

There will be times when a successful student needs to make a difficult decision. Should they do someone else's delegated tasks or risk getting a bad grade? The simple answer is that the student should pick up the slack to protect his or her own grade. The complicated answer is that picking up the slack can be a source of contention among group members who may feel like the student picking up the slack is too controlling and not allowing them a chance to do their work. Also, if it is apparent to the professor that only one student did all the work, there may be a deduction in points if part of the assignment requirements had to do with the process of working together.

BALANCE EXTRACURRICULAR & CURRICULAR ACTIVITIES

Part of getting the most out of college is becoming involved in an extracurricular activity. Extracurricular activities are school-sponsored organizations such as student government, athletics, academic clubs and organizations, service groups, and multicultural groups. Depending on the organization, the time commitment can be as little as an hour or two each month to as much as 10 or more hours per week. Students who partake in extracurricular activities find they have to make an extra effort to get everything done, but most will agree it is worth the effort. Extracurricular activities foster a sense of school pride and teach real-world skills, enhance experiences, develop self-awareness, and looks good on a resume.

AVOID PROCRASTINATING

When it comes to participating in extracurricular activities, students find that a big downfall is procrastination. They have so much to do that there is no time to waste. The best way to avoid this is to stick to a study schedule and to schedule free time so it does not get overlooked.

Make a List of Priorities

Students who successfully balance extracurricular and curricular activities know their priorities and are able to make quick decisions based on these priorities. For example, a student athlete puts her sport as one of her top priorities. To continue competing she knows that she needs to keep her grades up. This helps her overcome distractions when she is supposed to be studying. Another student may participate in student government. He knows he needs to stay healthy to be able to function well. During busy weeks it is easy for him to say no to his normal workout in lieu of something else, but he knows if he does he will feel crummy by the end of the day. The priority of feeling healthy helps him keep his scheduled workout.

Get a Tutor

Students who are involved in time-consuming extracurricular activities do not have time to mess around. Their participation in the activity relies on getting the grade, and if they are struggling in a class they need to explore the tutoring options offered at the university. Universities have a variety of tutoring options from single to once-a-week or more sessions. This scheduled tutoring time ensures students will get the help they need when they need it instead of wasting precious time struggling on their own.

Use University Enforced Study Sessions

Time-consuming extracurricular activities that are, such as sports may have team- or university-enforced study sessions. Students are required to attend, but of course no one can make them sit down and study. Successful students use this time to their advantage. They make sure they come prepared with a variety of work and get down to business so that when the session is over they can take a break and reward themselves for a job well done.

CASE STUDY: HOLLY A. TRACY-POTTER

Holly A. Tracy-Potter began her career at Dartmouth in October 1997 working in the Dean's office. She was on the "front line" interacting with students struggling with and/or celebrating their accomplishments. As an assistant to one of the upper-class deans, there were ample opportunities to lend an ear or shoulder.

In March 2002, Holly took an opportunity to move to the Academic Skills Center, where she assumed responsibility for directing the activities and programming of the Tutor Clearinghouse, a peer academic support network. Since that time, the level of activity has increased by 300 percent.

Holly's thoughts on student adjustment:

The whole transition to college life (including being away from their families and nuclear support system) is head-turning for students. Time management and the rigor of their coursework seem to trip up most first-year students.

Holly's thoughts on student surprises:

The amount of and difficulty of the work they will be facing is a huge surprise for students.

Holly's thoughts on student distractions and advice:

Distractions in the form of wanting to do/try everything that piques their interest are common. They must be intentional about it balancing their time by mapping out a schedule so that they see where conflicts will occur.

Holly's thoughts on important study tips:

Study early and often. Read the material ahead of lectures so they have some familiarity with the discussion topic. Review notes regularly with the aim of being able to synthesize the information in a meaningful way. Find study partners with whom you are comfortable working. It is best to identify individuals in all classes with whom you can work so that you develop a cohort of students who are working toward the same end. There is a good amount of research that supports group study environments. Peers supporting peers works wonders when trying to master complex material.

CASE STUDY: HOLLY A. TRACY-POTTER

Holly's thoughts on memories:

There is a student who has been working with me off and on who is struggling with the multiple things about which she is passionate. She's trying to devise a plan that will allow her to "have her cake and eat it too." Yet she realizes that she does not have the time to devote to everything; she's had to drop a course because she took on more than she could handle.

We regularly "check in." I suggested that she consider planning on having a day devoted to herself to think/plan/map out priorities and how she'll get to her goal. She needs to determine ahead of time what outcome she wants to see and then plan for that. There is myriad amount of research that suggests that multi-tasking is not efficient or effective. Her experience supports that theory. Planning is the only way she'll come close to being successful. Ironically, she wrote an open letter to first-year students this year about taking advantage of the services available to all students through the Tutor Clearinghouse. She knows what she has to do; she's just not quite there yet.

BALANCE SCHOOL & WORK

While it would be nice if every college student could say "school comes first" and the job is secondary, this is not the case for everyone. Some students have families to support and others simply could not afford tuition and living expenses if they did not also have a job, so in some cases, school and the job go hand in hand.

Students may think it would be ideal to attend college without having a job. Others have found that having a job helps them stay on task when they are studying and they use their scheduled work times as a motivator to get things done when they do have the time. Either way. students who have a job need to take extra care to balance it with their school work.

LOOK FOR ON-CAMPUS JOBS

One way successful students balance school and work is to look for jobs right on campus. These jobs may be more flexible than other jobs and the hours might fit in between classes. Plus, students who work on campus do not waste time commuting to a job elsewhere. There are numerous jobs available to students on most campuses. Some of these jobs or places to work include:

- Food service
- Security guards
- Janitorial services
- Fitness centers
- Computer labs
- Bookstores
- Research assistants
- Printing and copying centers
- Groundskeepers
- Libraries
- Department aides
- Day care centers
- IT services
- Residence halls
- Tutoring
- Professor and program assistants

STAY ORGANIZED TO STUDY ANYWHERE

Successful students who work while going to school know they need to be prepared to study during any spare time they find. This could be on the bus on the way to work, at work if it is slow, or during a spare 15 minutes when a lecture lets out early. To do this, successful students carry study materials with them.

Successful students also need to know where they are going to be and what they need to do. This requires them to keep a detailed schedule of work, classes, and study sessions. Successful working students also know they need to schedule free time so that they do not burn out from constantly working.

CUT BACK AS NEEDED

Even the most organized student will need to cut back working hours at certain times of the semester succeed in class. Mid-term and finals weeks can be stressful for every student and those who work will want to discuss this with their employers well in advance to be able to switch hours or take time off to study.

SURVIVING FINALS WEEK

Finals week can be bittersweet for many students. Yes, it is a sign that the semester is over and they are that much closer to graduation, but finals week can induce high stress and low tolerance for students. It does not have to be this way. Successful students know if they have kept up with their studies all semester; have kept their materials, study guides, study sheets, and returned assignments organized; and have stayed on a regular routine that involves healthy eating and exercise, finals week will be much less stressful than it is for those students who find they have to cram a few weeks or a whole semester's worth of work into the last two weeks.

ADJUST SCHEDULE

Successful students know they need to start preparation for finals week early. The first step is to adjust the schedule for final exams and due dates for projects, papers, and presentations. Successful students start by making a calendar that covers the final two weeks of the semester. Then they write in all exams and due dates. They also add in classes and other non-negotiable commitments. Next, they figure out how much time they will need to study for each exam and start filling in the study blocks. They should avoid starting studying more than one week in advance of the exam though, because they will likely forget some of the material first studied.

Here are some other hints to reduce the stress of finals weeks:

- **Take time off work** – this may need to be approved further in advance than two weeks.

- **Avoid skipping one class to study for another** – students who do this may miss important information about the upcoming exam.

- **Put priority on items that can be finished more than a week ahead of time**, such as papers and other written assignments, to leave the week before the exams open for studying.

- **This is the one time during a semester that students may need to forfeit large quantities of free time.** While it is important to take breaks and relax, a movie night may not be possible until after the exams.

Attend Study Sessions

Part of adjusting the schedule for successful students is considering the study sessions offered by the professors. These valuable resources may be overlooked by students because they do not have time to attend; they do not realize the valuable insight about the exam they will gain. Professors tend to be more candid about the format of the exam to students who make the effort to attend the study sessions. For example, the professor may give details such as how many essay questions will appear or the point values of each section of the test. Even if the professor is not candid about the exam at the study session, students who attend get a ready-made review which can only help them prepare.

Successful students take these study sessions seriously. They arrive prepared and ready to review:

- They study first so they have a basis for the information covered and so they can follow the information provided. Studying first also allows them to test themselves when other students ask questions.

- They arrive with a few questions of their own. Even if they do not get the chance to ask the questions, they have them ready in case no one else covers these specific topics.

- They arrive on time since professors may start with a prepared lecture that gives the condensed version of what will be on the exam before opening the session up for questions from the students.

STAY HEALTHY

With all of the extra work that goes into finals week, students look for ways to squeeze more time out of the day. One of the biggest mistakes students make when looking for ways to find more study time is to skip meals or regular workouts in lieu of studying. This is counter-productive because it can throw the body's system out of whack when its normal routine is disrupted. Instead, successful students put staying healthy at the top of their priority list. They:

- Eat healthy and balanced meals every day even if it means taking a little extra time to do so. Students who do not partake in a university food program may want to plan ahead and make some meals that can be frozen in individual servings so they can pop them in the microwave instead of cooking an entire meal.

- Continue their normal exercise routine. It gives them the energy needed to make it through the day.

- Get plenty of sleep. A tired brain cannot function efficiently.

Use exercise as a way to take a break. Instead of plopping down to watch television or surf the Internet for 20 minutes, they go for a walk or get up and stretch.

Pack healthy snacks and water for their study sessions so they are less tempted to binge on candy and other junk food.

Avoid Stress

Finals week can be stressful enough without the added stress of non school-related things. Successful students do their best to set aside these other distractions before they begin their finals week studying and testing schedule.

They ask family and significant others to be flexible and understanding about their busy weeks.

They take care of financial obligations such as paying bills before finals weeks begins.

They do a major cleaning of their dorm or apartment before starting their finals studying and testing schedule so they are not stressed about a messy home or tempted to clean instead of work.

They take plenty of breaks to clear their minds and rejuvenate themselves before starting another study session.

They plan a reward at the end of finals week so they have something to look forward to during the week.

They ask questions about their upcoming finals beforehand to get a better idea of the format of the test, the information that will be covered, and if there is a study guide available.

Stay Organized

Successful students attribute their success to staying organized even when they are busy. When they stay organized all semester they do not have to scramble at the last minute to find materials, recreate study sheets, and fill in missing notes. Instead, they have all of the information they need ready to go when it is time to study. They also:

- Plan ahead by making a list of the materials that will be needed for each class's exam and getting them all together.

- Take the time each night to gather the needed materials for exams and study sessions the next day.

- Plan to vary study materials by studying for several exams each day.

Remember Studying and Test-Taking Strategies

Successful students remember that in the grand scheme of things, the final exam is just another test. If they apply their normal studying and test-taking strategies they will be doing the best they can. Students can use their test-taking strategies along with the knowledge they have about the professor's testing style (from tests previous in the semester) to tailor their study sessions and prepare each testing strategy.

CASE STUDY: KAYLA VERDEGAN

Kayla Verdegan is a student at the University of Wisconsin Stout majoring in dietetics. She is involved with the track and field team and holds a work study position as an office assistant for the head track and field coach.

Kayla's thoughts on the learning style:

The hardest thing about studying in college is being able to set priorities and know what to study. Classes may have things due or tests at the same time in the semester. It must also be understood that it is nearly impossible to read everything teachers want you to and do all of the little stuff, but that doesn't mean don't do anything. Get big, graded assignments done first. Then if there's time do the other stuff; otherwise nothing will get done. For studying for quizzes and tests, knowing what to study can be hard. I try to anticipate what I think could be possible questions and the types of questions the particular professor is likely to ask. (I use previous tests or quizzes as a guide).

The biggest surprise for me was the amount of homework and how high expectations are. I came from high school where you could walk out of school with no homework and nothing to do because you get it all done in class or at school. At college it all has to be done on your own time.

Kayla's thoughts on distractions and balancing time:

Some of the things that tend to pull me away from my studies include: track (sports), social activities, and events constantly going on, roommates, and the Internet is a big one. Since I have to do homework on the computer and wireless Internet is all around, I check e-mail, check Facebook, and look up information that does not pertain to my studies. It is hard for me to balance my time. I try to plan my day in advance and have time set aside to get certain stuff done. I then reward myself when I get things done by being able to attend an event or doing something fun. I have to be disciplined and tell myself that I can't do something else until what needs to get done is done. It's all about prioritizing for me.

Kayla's thoughts on mistakes:

I was independent. I felt like help was for those who were failing classes or just didn't have a clue about the material. Instead, help is for everyone; that's what it's there for. I

CASE STUDY: KAYLA VERDEGAN

was told this since I started college and it started to sink in a little bit about two months into college. It actually hit me at the beginning of the second semester of my freshman year when my psychology professor just laid it all out for me and gave some tips.

Kayla's thoughts on hindsight:

You can't do it for a longer duration of time than you would your favorite activity. For example, if I loved basketball I would play it for a long amount of time and quite often, but not more than three or four hours at one time. I would find myself not moving from my desk for up to 10 hours at a time (except to go to the bathroom) just trying to study and get everything done. The longer I sat there the less productive I would become. I found out that I needed to take a break to get away from it and refresh my mind a bit so I could return to it refreshed and productive. Compare this to basketball. If I played basketball for 10 hours at one time I would get so fatigued, bored, and sick of it that I would hardly be able to do it anymore.

Kayla's thoughts on figuring out study tricks:

Start early. I found that starting to study early helps me to retain and learn the information better. Doing a little at a time, understanding, and then reviewing later helps me understand the information better and saves me time and hassle. It works better than trying to overload the brain in one night.

For homework I work best by getting something done early; it relieves the stress of getting it done at the last minute. I can revise if I want or if I think of something better to add or say or find an answer later I will have time to change it. As for studying, itself I find that writing things down helps me study.

Putting the pieces of the puzzle together in my mind helps me learn the concepts instead of just memorizing and dumping the information. I like to be able to picture what's going on and how it applies to me.

Kayla's thoughts on challenges:

I think the best thing a student can do is go to class! Being independent now, it is easy to just say, "I'm pretty tired; I'll just read the book" or "I'll just talk to someone later." I find that by going to class I'm able to get all of the information and maybe a story to help me remember the information. Another thing that challenges students to get good grades is devoting the time necessary to do their studying and/or homework. This has to do with time management and prioritizing their social life.

CASE STUDY: KAYLA VERDEGAN

Colleges recommend devoting two to three hours per week per every hour spent in class that week. This is rather demanding and students may choose not to put this time in and their grades suffer because of it.

Kayla's thoughts on routines:

I have a fairly consistent study routine. I plan out my day in advance. I try to treat school like a job. I wake up early as I would if I were going to work. From that time I am considered "at work." Whether I am in class or doing homework, that time is devoted to school. Of course, I have lunch and am walking to and from class, but for eight hours of work time, school is my job. When those eight hours are up, I do whatever else needs to be done such as my sport, or an event, or something.

Kayla's thoughts on obstacles:

The biggest obstacle for me when it comes to studying is time. My solution comes down to three words: balance, moderation, and variety. Everyone needs balance in their life; students can't be expected to study in all of their free time.

STUDY ABROAD

Studying abroad is a fantastic opportunity that should not be overlooked by anyone who wants to get the most out of his or her college career. Study abroad programs have benefits for students regardless of their majors, and there are now a variety of options for lengths and types of programs making it is possible for students to fit a program into their college schedules.

UNDERSTAND THE BENEFIT

Students who choose to study abroad get more than the college credits they earn while abroad. One of the biggest benefits is the travel and opportunity to meet new people. It also looks good on a resume. Successful students who have studied abroad also like that they were able to:

- **Learn or practice a second language.** Students who want to learn a new language find that full immersion in a country that speaks the language is the best way to become fluent.

- **Learn about different cultures.** Many study abroad programs also allow the students to live with a family in the country which gives them first-hand experience about the people and customs of the country.

❧ **Increase their independence and confidence.** Surviving in a completely new environment has a positive effect on self-confidence!

❧ **Better appreciate their home country.** Students who study abroad will soon be able to identify the comforts of home that they miss the most — even those who are not necessarily homesick.

❧ **Understand the skills needed to function in a global economy.** Students may be offered the opportunity to participate in an internship or volunteer position so that they can see first hand how their business or area of study differs from that at home.

Students who study abroad also tend to enroll in classes that make use of the location. For example, studying European architecture is much more meaningful when the student can look at the examples first hand instead of just looking at photographs.

Choose a Program

There are so many different types of study abroad programs it is difficult to know where to start. Some of them involve one concentrated class for three weeks between semesters. Others are for a few months in the summer and others are for a complete semester or year in a select location. It is important to start this search early on in college so students have time to apply and complete any prerequisites necessary before embarking on their journey.

There are four types of academic programs that students can choose. The first type is a full semester or year when the students go to the destination and take a full load of credits. The second type of program is the concentrated class where a professor will take one class of students to a relevant location. They will complete the coursework and do supplementary activities relating to the location during a break in the semesters — typically for two or three weeks. The third type of program is a summer program where students may take a lighter load of classes and may spend more time participating in an internship or volunteer position at the same time.

The first place to look for a study abroad program is with the university. The Dean of Students office or academic advisors can lead students in the right direction. If the college or university does not have their own study abroad program, they may cooperate with another school that does have one. Other places to look are reference books in the library and Web sites.

Students who have successfully chosen a study abroad program suggest looking at the following characteristics when choosing a program. Students should:

- Inquire about credit transfer to ensure they will get credit for all of the classes they take.

- Look at the course offerings to make sure they will have enough classes that interest them and that fit into their major.

- Find out who teaches the classes – professors from the United States who are also participating in the program or foreign professors. Both options have their pros and cons.

- Find out about available housing and where it will be in proximity to the location of the classes.

- Find out about tuition, living expenses and extra fees.

Other considerations for choosing a program include the destination, the duration, and when during the year the program is available. Some programs require a certain number of undergraduate credits before students can apply for the program so this is also an important consideration.

Above all, it is important to talk to students who have been through the program to get a first-hand view of the strengths and weaknesses of the program.

Make it Count

The biggest mistake students make with their study abroad programs is they do not capitalize on the opportunity as much as they should. There are different ways to do this.

First, students should research their destination before they go so they know where they want to visit while they are there. This can be done with a travel book, on the Internet, or by talking to people who have been there.

Second, students should do as much as possible while there to immerse themselves in the customs and traditions of the location — frequenting the places the "locals" go.

Finally, students need to use their opportunity to their advantage when they return home. They can do this by:

- Visiting an academic advisor to schedule classes for the upcoming semester at home. Successful students consider the classes they took during the study abroad program so they can avoid taking similar classes again.

- Seeing a career counselor at the university to help them distinguish the study abroad experience on their resume.

- Mentoring students who are deciding whether they want to study abroad and helping them choose a program that is right for them.

Part 6

Avoiding Studying Downfalls

Keeping Up With It All

Even the most successful, studious, and conscientious students will find themselves in situations where they require extra help. There will be semesters that require obscene amounts of writing because of the mix of classes and there will be semesters that require tons of reading because of the mix of classes. There will also be semesters difficult semesters because all of the classes are extremely demanding. When this happens, all students, even the most successful students, need to know what to do to survive and succeed.

UTILIZE OFFERED RESOURCES

The university wants its students to succeed so they have a wide variety of helpful resources available to them. While they may "advertise" these resources, it is not feasible for the university to tell students about every resource available to them should they need it in the future. This leaves it up to students to investigate on their own to find the resources that best suit their needs.

GET INVOLVED WITH ACADEMIC DEPARTMENTS

Successful students are involved with their major and minor departments. They attend department functions, join the academic organizations, and apply for the academic honor societies. They get to know the professors and other students in the department in a different setting. This is beneficial for the successful student in a number of ways:

- Students get to know the professors which will help them choose which classes they want to take in the future.

- Professors get to know the students and may be more flexible or understanding when the student needs assistance.

- Students can ask other students in the department for advice on interesting classes, suggestions for certain types of projects, and help getting through specific classes.

- Professors are more likely to share information about "hidden" resources to students they know on a more personal level.

- Students will have opportunities to help choose and plan department-sponsored events.

Frequent Tutoring & Writing Centers

Successful students know there is nothing wrong with getting help when they need it. This is why they know where to find the tutoring center and the writing center. These centers can assist students on a one-time basis or they can set up regular sessions throughout the semester. Successful students like these opportunities because:

- It is beneficial to get an opinion from a "fresh set of eyes" when writing a paper.

- Tutors can help students detect errors they did not realize they were making.

- It is beneficial to be able to talk through a problem with someone who knows what they are doing.

- These services can give them an extra edge to stand out in class.

- These services may be free for registered students.

Students who need extra help and who are not sure where to look should consult their professors for ideas for tutors and other student services.

LOOK FOR OLD TEST RESOURCES

Another valuable resource that goes unnoticed by many students is a compilation of old tests submitted by professors. These resources may be housed in the library or they may be found in department offices and lounges. They are beneficial because students can use these tests to see the types of tests the professor writes including the format, types of questions, and level of detail. The other benefit is that these tests may serve as study guides or practice tests. When using these resources, however, students should:

- Ask the professor if his or her submitted tests remain relevant to the class because the professor may have completely revamped their class.

- Avoid relying solely on these tests as a study guide because they may not cover all of the information needed to succeed on current tests.

- Avoid looking at tests for the same class from different professors since it will not be useful to them unless the course has a universal test for all sections.

- Realize that even if the professor has not submitted tests for their specific course, they may be able to benefit by looking at other tests submitted by the professor to get a sense of their testing style.

FIND OUT ABOUT ELECTRONIC STUDY AIDS

The library and media centers at universities have electronic study aids such as practice tests, study guides, and other supplementary materials that can help students study and understand the materials. Successful students locate these by asking their professor or the media specialists at the library.

Visit Counseling Centers

Counseling centers are useful for students. Universities may have one counseling center with different departments within or they may have several different counseling centers including general counseling, study skill counseling, financial counseling, and career counseling. Counseling centers are not just for students who need help with personal or emotional problems. Successful students have found that counseling centers can help with:

- Test anxiety
- Financial concerns
- Substance abuse
- Adjustment issues
- Stress management
- Time management and organization
- Career choices and preparation
- Conflict resolution (between roommates or friends)

- Learning disabilities
- Peer assistance groups
- Crisis assistance
- Multicultural issues
- Couple and relationship issues

Read Professor Evaluations

One advantage college students have is the ability to choose their schedule down to which professor they take, especially in classes that have multiple sections. Successful students like this because they can find professors that teach to their preferred learning style. One way they can find professors is by looking at the university-sponsored professor evaluations which contain student comments about the professor and the class.

LEARN HOW TO ACCESS DATABASES OR RESEARCH

The library or media centers have numerous databases available to students for research. These databases can range from general research tools to subject-specific databases. With the advances in technology, these databases are also normally offered on the Web for student use outside of the library.

SEARCH FOR SPECIALTY LIBRARIES & COLLECTIONS

While universities have well-known main libraries there may also be less-publicized specialty libraries or collections. These specialty libraries and collections may be student resource rooms in an academic department or they may be housed in rooms or offices in administrative buildings on campus. Successful students locate these by asking or by wandering campus and taking note of potentially useful resources they find.

USE DISABILITY SERVICES

Successful students with disabilities can access services to help them in needed areas. Students who wish to use these services need to apply and be accepted to the disability services programs. After acceptance they may meet with a program counselor so they can decide which support services are necessary and available. In some cases, students with temporary injuries may also be able to access these services during their recovery.

These resources may include:

- Classroom modifications
- Counseling
- Tutoring services
- Books on tape
- Testing modifications
- Document conversion
- Access assistance
- Sign language

CASE STUDY: JUSTIN BAER,

Justin Baer was a "B" student in high school and ended up graduating from cum laude and with honors from New York University in 2004. He discovered the secrets to studying in college and has designed and marketed a DVD called *Cracking College: The Seven Secrets of Savvy Students.*

Justin's thoughts on student adjustment:

Students are not prepared to handle a balance between social life and academics. The academics are more challenging than what they are used to and they are now also responsible for themselves. They no longer have teachers or parents riding them to show up and be responsible. The combinations of these struggles cause a trend of downfall of college success.

Justin's thoughts on student surprises:

I think that the biggest surprise is the responsibility that they now have to take on. In high school, if they had missing home work the teacher would call home or pull the student aside. In college it's up to the student.

Justin's thoughts on important study tips:

Use all of the resources available — tutors and writing centers in particular.

If students do a little more legwork up front they'll do less later. For example, students who work ahead on their papers can take them to the writing center for help on them. This would not be possible if they waited until the night before to write. You can't wait until the last minute, but you can get the help you need.

We have a segment in the video about the University of Maryland. They have a school-sponsored repository of old exams for student use, yet 85 percent of students surveyed didn't know it was there.

Justin's thoughts on student challenges.

Students struggle in classes but they don't realize that if they take a little effort when scheduling they might experience fewer challenges during the semester. They can research the professor and the classes to find formats and themes that interest them instead of randomly choosing classes and hoping for the best.

USE THE FIRST YEAR TO PREPARE FOR THE REST

Successful students know they need to make the most of their freshman year to help them prepare for their future classes, which will presumably get more difficult and demanding as they go along. There are things first-year students can do — from scheduling to taking an afternoon to explore the campus — that will help them succeed in the future.

TAKE A WRITING CLASS

Any college student or graduate knows that college requires substantial amounts of writing in different styles and formats. There are college students who do not know the basics of writing a good paper; those who can write well will stand out to their professors. The best way to do this is start early with a college-level writing class and continue to use the skills learned in this class. Students who are skilled writers and comfortable with the process will fare much better than those who are not. While it may sound overwhelming, students should ask around to find a demanding writing professor and take that class the first year. The writing skills acquired will be indispensable for the next three-plus years of college.

Take a Speech Class

Many students suffer stage fright. They dread the mere thought of taking a speech class. The truth is, however, they will be required in the vast majority of their classes to make a speech or presentation. Whether formal or informal, practiced or impromptu, the sooner they learn how to do it the better they will fare when these assignments arise.

There is nothing worse for a student than knowing what they want to say but being unable to get their point across because they do not know how to prepare or deliver it effectively. As with writing, speaking well comes with practice. The best way to start is in a class where they expect mistakes and will give tips and tricks to avoid them in the future.

Take a Campus Tour with an Upperclassman

Successful students find an upperclassman to take them around campus and share their knowledge about resources, social destinations, professors, majors, extracurricular activities, shortcuts, and campus safety. This tour can be with a residence hall advisor, a friend, or someone from the student's intended major department. It may also be a member of a group or organization the new student wants to join. The campus tour can help the first-year student better acclimate to campus life, helping ease the transition to this new lifestyle.

KEEP IT REAL

College can be so overwhelming for some students that they may soon find themselves doing just enough to get by. This is all right to get through stressful times, but students who constantly have to do this may find they are not staying true to themselves. College is a time of growing and maturing as much as it is a time of learning and earning a degree,. Successful students make sure they stay true to themselves.

EXAMINE VALUES

Successful students periodically examine their values. This could be as simple as making sure they are spending enough time with their friends and family to as complex as making sure they are being honest in their work. By examining their values, successful students help themselves stay true to their priorities. They stay motivated because they know they are on the right track.

One way they examine their values is by looking at their lives to make sure they have their priorities in order and if they are not, to make changes. They can also evaluate if what they are doing is making them happy. If it is not, they need to figure out what they need to do to add more enjoyment to their lives.

Define Personal Success

Successful students also need to define for themselves at what point they will be successful. For some, it is earning straight A's in college and graduating with high honors. For others, personal success is not only earning their degree but also completing a certain type of volunteer work. Other students may deem themselves successful if they have made an impact on the campus or student body while in school. Personal success is different for everyone, and those who define it for themselves will be able to judge whether they are successful students.

Make Goals

Students avoid setting goals because they do not know what they want out of college or they do not know how to set goals. Some simply are overwhelmed with the idea of setting goals and then having to stick to them. It is important for students to remember, however, that goals can be modified as their lives change. It is just important to set them to have something to work toward.

- Goals help with motivation because they give the students an end point to work toward.

- Goals help students make difficult decisions. If the decision hinders progress toward an important goal, it is the wrong decision.

- Goals help students with their priorities. Again, if something hinders progress toward a goal, it should not be high on the priority list.

Setting goals can be overwhelming, but here are a few tips successful students use when setting goals:

📚 The goal needs to be desirable to the student. Students may set goals because they sound good or they think they will make others happy; these goals will fall by the wayside and will not be big motivators if the student does not want to reach them.

📚 The goal needs to be achieved in connection with other goals. For example, a full-time student who has one goal of graduating in four years will likely not be able to also fulfill a goal that requires him or her to work a full forty-hour week as well. These two goals are not compatible with each other.

📚 The goals should be positive and explain what the students want to do, not what they want to avoid.

📚 The goals should be specific so the students will know when they reach them.

📚 The goals should be written down on paper and kept visible such as on a bulletin board or on a home page on the Internet.

STAY CONNECTED TO THE "REAL WORLD"

Students who live and work on campus can easily lose sight of the real world. It is easy to work, study, go to class, and play without paying attention to what is going on in the real world unless a professor brings up a current event. Successful students make an effort to read the newspaper, current event magazines, news sites on the Internet, or to watch news programs at least once a week to keep in touch with what is happening in the world around them. Keeping in touch with current events will help them apply the concepts they learn in class to current events, not just what is happening on campus.

Examine Majors and Minors Frequently

Students may start college with an idea of what they want to do when they are finished, but the number of students who actually finish with their first major is quite low. It is not unusual for students to change majors, decide on a double major or add an extra minor during their education. Most students agree it is better to add an extra semester of schooling to change a major than to finish with a degree they do not want to use. Successful students know to look for the following signs that they may be in the wrong major:

- They do not enjoy many — or any — of their classes in their majors.

- They cannot decide on a job that they would both be qualified for and enjoy.

- They tried an internship and they were miserable.

- They do not feel challenged.

- They complain about their studies.

- They believe fellow classmates are much more interested in the subject matter than they are.

- Their priorities have changed and the current major no longer helps them work toward meeting their goals.

Know When to Transfer

It is not unusual for students to transfer from one university to another to finish their schooling. There are a number of reasons for a transfer including being closer to home, being at the same school as a significant other, finding a school that has a better program for the intended major, or simply wanting a change of scenery. Successful students know how to recognize the signs that they need to transfer to a different school:

- A different school has a more prestigious program for their intended major.

- The only reason the student is not changing majors is because the current school does not offer the intended major.

- The current school is becoming unaffordable.

There are also reasons why a college transfer is not necessarily the best choice. Students who are having a difficult time adjusting to college life may think it will be easier at a different school when perhaps they just need to give it a little time. Some students may look at transferring to a new school to be closer to friends; while this is not necessarily a bad idea, it could be if the new school does not have the right program for the student.

Once the decision to transfer has been made, for whatever reason, it is important the student takes his or her time to be sure to find the right school.

CASE STUDY: TERI MCKEAN

Teri McKean is a graduate student at the University of Illinois Chicago studying for her masters of social work – mental health with an expected graduation of May 2008. She completed her undergraduate degree at the University of Wisconsin Oshkosh in May 1999 with a bachelor of arts degree in journalism and health promotion.

Teri's thoughts on the learning style:

CASE STUDY: TERI MCKEAN

As an undergraduate the biggest surprise was that I actually had to study. As a graduate student it was that I was no longer "studying" to memorize, but to understand theories and concepts and how those can be applied to my work.

Teri's thoughts on distractions and balancing time:

The biggest distractions are my children, cleaning, and wanting to just hang out. I have a rigid schedule of how I spend my time. Rarely do I stray from it.

Teri's thoughts on mistakes:

I majored in the wrong thing as an undergraduate, but I realized it the spring semester of my senior year, and I wasn't going to change majors at that point. I should have noticed the warning signs while I was studying and preparing for classes — this wasn't what I wanted to do with my life. Instead, I just plugged through the material. I couldn't fix that decision, but I made the best of the situation, graduating with honors so I had a base to start with. Eventually I went back to graduate school, and feel my undergraduate education and study habits have come in handy. I did appreciate the writing and interviewing skills I gained. They have been so valuable! The lesson here is to make sure you get plenty of experiences in college, not only in your major area, and use those four years to figure out your values and what you hope to accomplish in life — more than a salary.

Teri's thoughts on hindsight:

I wish I would have known that it was more than just memorizing material. As you progress through subjects and coursework, you have to find a way to conceptualize what you are learning and how to apply it to the rest of your life and your. I have a classmate who is not reading material for our class "because we're not being tested on it." I want to be able to have a knowledgeable conversation about the material and understand why the professor thinks it is important to the class. They don't pick random material to make you read, but stuff that fits into the objectives of the class.

Teri's thoughts on figuring out study tricks:

The best tip is prioritizing what needs to be read for that week. You might try asking the professor to pick that out for you. Another tip while reading or learning material is to find the stuff that challenges you and spend more time on it. If the material comes easily to you, then you aren't learning anything new.

CASE STUDY: TERI MCKEAN

Teri's thoughts on memories:

On two different occasions I wasn't looking at the syllabus well and read the wrong week's material. In one case, that wasn't a huge deal, I just didn't have a lot to say during discussion. In the other, it was bad since we had weekly quizzes on the readings.

Teri's' thoughts on challenges:

The biggest challenge is balance. Everyone can learn the material, either through their own hard work or with the help of tutors and study groups. Finding a way to balance their time is hard. A schedule helps with that.

As a graduate student, it is finding the time to keep up with the volume of material assigned. I also have to set priorities on a regular basis and sneak in chapters or articles on the train, between classes, or while eating a breakfast.

Teri's thoughts on routines:

I do all my studying at night. I have class twice a week. My study week begins on Wednesday or Thursday as I start to read the material for the following Tuesday's classes. I then continue to plug away until the following Tuesday when I finish up the reading for that Thursday's class. If papers or assignments are due, they take top priority, and I try to fit in time to create an outline or research in the two to three weeks before the due date to give myself enough time.

Teri's thoughts on obstacles:

My biggest obstacle is e-mail. I want to check it on a regular basis, and my computer is located in the same place as my desk. It's so tempting to stop reading and send out a quick e-mail. We all know people send you links and you check your bank balance or the weather forecast. I have to give myself a few minutes at the start to check e-mail and then force myself to wait until I'm done to check it again!

BOOST YOUR CONCENTRATION

It happens at the worst times — even for successful students: concentration levels drop when students need it most, usually the day before a big exam or when they need to finish an assignment. There are ways, however, that students can give their concentration a boost.

KEEP A LIST

A big reason students have difficulty concentrating is they start thinking about all of the other things they need to do. This could be what they need to get at the grocery store or ideas for their next project. It could be who they need to e-mail and why. Successful students have found that when their minds start wandering, the best thing for them to do is keep a notebook handy so they can make a list of whatever is trying to take over their thoughts. If they keep thinking about the grocery store, they quickly make a list. If they keep thinking about e-mail, they make a list of who they want to e-mail when they are done. The list is there and waiting for them so they can stop thinking about it.

Diagnose Which Classes Cause the Most Concentration Problems

Certain classes may cause the concentration problems during the actual class. While students cannot change the time of the class, they can adjust their schedule to help with in-class concentration. If the class is at the time of day when the student tends to be tired, they can try taking a quick walk or having a light, healthy snack to give them an extra boost of energy. If the class is at the end of a long day, the student can try taking a break from studies and other schoolwork before the class.

If a student is having concentration problems while studying for a certain class, the student can do several things to help boost his or her concentration during study blocks. First, the student should plan to study for this class when he or she has more energy. Second, the student should try to study for the class in short increments and take frequent brief breaks. Finally, the student may want to join a study group for the class to try to study the material more actively.

Remove External Distractions

Another common cause of a lack of concentration is the external distractions that can pull the student's attention away from the subject. In class, students who sit near the door may be distracted by people and noises in the hallways. Students sitting near windows may be distracted by the outdoors. Students sitting in the back of the class may get distracted by other students in class. What is the solution? Successful students sit in the front of the class, especially in courses that tend to challenge their concentration.

External distractions while studying can be household chores, roommates, television, and the Internet. Students can avoid these by not studying at home and keeping the Internet off. They can also look for quiet places to study that do not have much people traffic.

AVOID MULTI-TASKING

Reading and walking on the treadmill may sound like a resourceful idea, but students who do this do not get as much as they should out of their reading or their workout. While those who multitask get more done, it may not be done as well as if they had concentrated on just one task at a time.

SET MINI GOALS

Students who have a difficult time concentrating may also want to try setting mini goals to help them get their work accomplished. Here is how it works:

- A mini goal should be achievable in a relatively short amount of time (10 to 15 minutes).

- It should be specific. "Read more for the next few minutes" is not specific. "Read the next section in the chapter and answer the relevant questions on the study guide" is specific.

- There should be a reward — take a break, have a snack, check e-mail, or chat with a friend. The reward should be quick as well so the student can get back on task for the next mini goal.

A whole series of mini goals will accomplish more than simply saying "I need to read this entire chapter" and daydreaming the whole time.

When All Else Fails...

Take a break. A lack of concentration is the student's brain telling him or her that it needs a break, so at this point it is a better use of time for the student to give in and do something else for a while.

IMPROVE MEMORY

There will be classes that require memorization. While it is tempting for students to do the minimum to get a decent grade, they need to look at why the class is full of memorization. These classes may be prerequisites for a variety of classes because the information memorized in the class will be applied and used in later classes. Examples include anatomy and physiology for pre-medicine and nursing students or grammar for English majors. Successful students know that remembering things just long enough to get the information onto the test paper is not enough. They take action to improve their memory.

Successful students know that even if their memory is not the best, they have the ability to improve it. They also know this process is not easy, but they are willing to work to get to where they want to be.

MAKE A CONSCIOUS EFFORT

One way to improve memory is to make a conscious effort to do so. Students who tell themselves "I need to remember this," or "I have a good memory; it will be okay," actually trick themselves into remembering things they may not have remembered before. Simply telling the brain that this is important enough to remember gives the brain a cue to help recall the information when it is needed.

This works best for incidental items such as finding the car keys, remembering phone numbers and addresses, and noting a specific date. While this is not necessarily going to help a student remember all of the information for a test, it is an important start.

EXERCISE THE BRAIN

The brain is not a muscle, but it will function better if it is exercised on a regular basis. College students may argue their brains are exercised enough as it is, but it does not hurt to participate in some fun and games. Successful students know that working on word, logic, and number puzzles helps to keep the brain working and improves memory as well.

REPEAT AND RECITE

One of the best ways to remember things is to practice the repeat and recite method. This can be practiced with little things such as a grocery list or a list of supplies. Practicing with incidental items will help the student to use the repeat and recite method while studying.

For studying, students can use flash cards and other active study strategies, but they should work in an area where they can actually speak the information to help them remember it.

CREATE ACRONYMS

Students who are trying to remember a specific list or words, the steps to a procedure, or a specific theory or rule can use acronyms. Acronyms take the first letter of each word (or important word) and create a word or short phrase out of the initials. Once students have studied the acronym a few times, they will remember the words that go along with each initial. Here are some examples:

- **FACE:** This can help music students remember the notes on the treble staff.

- **HOMES:** The names of the Great Lakes: Huron, Ontario, Michigan, Erie, and Superior.

- **NEWS:** The directions on a compass: North, East, South, and West.

- **ROY G BIV:** The colors of the rainbow: Red, Orange, Yellow, Green, Blue, Indigo, and Violet.

VISUALIZE THE INFORMATION

Students who can put an outrageous or silly visual with the information will be able to remember the information through the visualization. For example, when trying to remember the capitol of Pennsylvania, a student may make the visualization of a big, hairy pen and think of the sentence, "My HARR-y PENN is BiG", to help them remember Harrisburg, Pennsylvania.

Another example of this theory is associating a person's name with their appearance or personality (i.e a happy person named Mary could be remembered at "Merry Mary"). It helps people recall other people's names and can be successful as long as they do not share their associations with that person since their outrageousness might be taken the wrong way. You can also associate the person's name (or any other important information you want to remember about that person) with your personal goals -- "This is Mike. He went to London last year and I plan on going next year." This association helps Mike stick out in your mind and you will likely remember other details about him as well.

This principle can be applied to any topic, but it works best when students have to associate information with a key word or phrase such as a date and its events or a person and his or her significance. As long as the picture is outrageous enough to stand out in the student's memory and has enough clues to be associated with the right key words, it will be a good way to help remember the clues. It takes time to come up with the visualizations, but this skill becomes easier with practice.

Write Sentences

Writing sentences can help students remember things in two ways. If students need to remember how to spell a difficult word, they could make a sentence using each of the letters as a first letter for the words in the sentence. When they remember the sentence, they will be able to spell the word.

- **MISSPELL:** Many Infants Suddenly Spit Peas Everywhere Long and Low.

- **DICTIONARY:** Did I Count The Ice On Nanna's Old Road Yet?

- **FELLOW:** For Everyone Leaving, Let's Order Watermelon.

- **DESSERT** (often confused with Desert): Dads Eat Strawberry Shortcake Even when Running out of Time.

The other way sentences can work to help students remember information is similar to how acronyms work by taking the first letter of each word in a list and using that letter to be the first letter of the word in a sentence. For example:

- Kingdom, Phylum, Class, Order, Family, Genus, Species: Kind Pat Can Only Find his Gigantic Suitcase.

Mercury, Venus, Earth, Mars, Jupiter, Saturn, Uranus, Neptune: My Very Energetic Mom Just Serve Us Nectarines.

Successful students have found this helpful when they need to remember a series or a list. They can study the list with the sentence and then eventually move to studying the sentence while recalling the list.

RHYME TO REMEMBER

There are times when a simple rhyme explaining the rule or date will help the student. There are plenty of rhymes already in use but students may also want to make up their own to make it relevant to the topic they are studying. For example:

"I" before "E" except after "C" or when sounding like "A" as in neighbor or weigh.

In fourteen-hundred-and-ninety-two, Columbus sailed the ocean blue.

OVERLOAD THE SENSES

A final way to help improve memory is to overload the senses. When students have important information to remember for an exam, they should apply the information to as many senses as possible. The more senses they involve in studying the information, the more likely they are to remember it. An example is to create a visualization of the material, link it to a tangible object, and imagine what it smells like. By doing this, students can recall the image, the tangible object, or the smell and will likely recall the information that goes with it.

IMPROVE VOCABULARY

While in college, students start developing their vocabulary to be more professional and educated. Part of this comes from taking classes and learning the terms that go along with their area of study, but successful students can go a little further by taking action to develop their vocabulary even more.

SUBSCRIBE TO A WORD OF THE DAY E-MAIL

Since most students are online at least once a day anyway, some students like to subscribe to a word of the day e-mail (found in several places on the Web) so they have easy access to a new word each day. The key to making this work is reading the e-mail and usage examples and then making it a point to use the word at least once each day (more if possible).

This same idea can be used by randomly picking a word out of the dictionary or by getting a word of the day calendar. To make it even more fun and beneficial the student can challenge roommates and friends to use the word and then talk about how each were able to use the word that day.

LEARN ROOTS, PREFIXES, AND SUFFIXES

Much of the English language is based on Greek and Latin roots. Additionally, many words contain prefixes and suffixes that are common to the language. People who understand the meaning of these roots, prefixes, and suffixes can decipher the general meaning of new words without consulting a dictionary. Here are some meanings and examples of Greek and Latin roots, prefixes, and suffices:

- **Ali:** Other. Alias, Alibi.

- **Amor:** Love, Liking. Amorous, Enamored.

- **Dura:** Lasting. Duration.

- **Man:** Hand. Manuel, Manicure.

- **Vive:** Life. Revive, Vivid.

- **Ambi:** Both. Ambidextrous.

- **Con:** With. Connected, Conspire.

- **Inter:** Between. Interstate.

- **Mono:** One. Monologue, Monogamy.

- **Cide:** Kill. Suicide.

- **Ectomy:** Cut. Appendectomy.

KEEP A LIST OF NEW WORDS

Students who are serious about learning new words keep a list of new words they encounter so when they have time they can look them up in the dictionary. Some students keep this list in a notebook so they have room to write in the definition as well as usage examples. This way they can study these new words and become familiar enough with them to actually use them.

Read

A student must be exposed to a word several times before he or she will be able to remember it and use it properly. This is the reason that the more they read, the more words they will learn. Some students like to read the dictionary when they have time or are taking a break from their studies. They find words and their meanings fascinating. It does not have to be the dictionary, though. Students who read fiction, newspapers, and magazines will also benefit by increasing their vocabulary as well.

Play

Word games such as Scrabble and crossword puzzles challenge the students' vocabularies and force them to learn about new words to succeed at the game.

STAY MOTIVATED

College is hard work — so hard, in fact, that some students just want to give up and have fun for a while. While taking a night off here and there may not to be detrimental to a student's college education, doing it consistently might be. Even successful students have occasions where they lack motivation to do their school work. It is how they manage these instances of low motivation that sets them apart from other students.

EXAMINE LACK OF MOTIVATION

Successful students first examine the reason they lack motivation to study. When they find out why, they will better know how to fix the problem.

- A lack of motivation due to not being interested in the classes may mean the student needs to reevaluate his or her course of study.

- A lack of motivation because the student does not enjoy a particular class may mean the student should decide if he or she needs to be taking the class. If it is not a required class, it may be worth dropping it.

🕮 A lack of motivation resulting from being exhausted may mean the student needs to reorganize his or her schedule or adopt healthier habits.

🕮 A lack of motivation stemming from personal or relationship issues may mean that the student should look into counseling.

Avoid Relying on Other People

An important lesson that successful students learn early on is they cannot rely on other people to motivate them, remind them, or force them to get their work done. That does not happen at the college level. Some students struggle with the adjustment process of no longer being monitored by their parents who remind them to study and take care of other necessities. Additionally, college professors are not going to hound students to get their work done or call them in for meetings if it looks like they are falling behind like high school teachers do. It is up to the student to make the time to study and then use that time for effective studying.

Stay Positive and Keep Things in Perspective

Another reason students may lose motivation is if they are so overwhelmed that they feel like nothing they do will make a difference. If they have a tough class that they have been struggling with all semester, they may lose the motivation to put the necessary time into the final exam because they do not feel like they have the ability to learn the material.

Successful students have learned it is important to put things into perspective. They may want to go out with their friends instead of staying in to study for that last final. They know that if they do not do well on the final they may have to retake the class, so they have to decide if one night out is worth retaking an entire class. They are in college; they know there will be something to do the following night anyway. By putting things in perspective, they can motivate themselves to study when they need to get it done.

MAKE LISTS

Some students work best when they can visualize what they have done and what they have left to do. A good motivator for these people is to write lists. The best way to do this is to write each item as a specific task — easily identified when it is complete. The successful student takes pride in crossing the completed task off the list. Seeing the list of things left to do shrink is a big motivator to finish it all. There is no better feeling for list makers than to have an empty to-do list!

START SMALL

Even with all of these tips, there may be times when successful students are unable to motivate themselves to do what needs to be done. This is when it is time for students to trick themselves into working. Here is how it works:

A successful student may put off starting an assignment for a variety of reasons. She knows she needs to at least get a start on it, but it is her evening to relax. She has about 25 minutes until her favorite television show starts. She tells herself she needs to sit down and read through the assignment sheet and make a plan to complete the assignment before she watches her show. This small task does not sound so bad, and she knows if she gets right on task she can have it done within about 15 minutes. She finds her materials, sits down at the table, and begins reading the assignment sheet.

At this point, one of three things can happen:

 Situation A. The student reads through the sheet, jots down questions, and makes a plan. She is done in 15 minutes and has a solid idea of what needs to be done to complete the project.

 Situation B. The student reads through the sheet, jots down questions, and makes a plan. She then realizes she already knows what prompt she wants to use because one popped out at her when she was reading through them. She initially thought about three possible topics that might work depending on the information available. She looks at the clock and sees she has ten minutes until her show starts so she logs on to the library's online catalog to see what types of information would be available for her possible topics to help her decide. She knows she does not need to make her decision right away, but she has things to think about to get the project moving in her brain.

 Situation C. The student reads through the sheet, but as she is doing so she realizes she does not understand the prompt and how it relates to the course and the topics discussed in class. She writes several questions on the sheet as she reads through it and then double checks her professor's office hours to see when she can plan to go ask him or her about the assignment.

Whichever situation occurred, the student accomplished something that night. In situation B, she tricked herself into completing more than she planned. In situation C, she was relieved she had taken the time to read through the assignment sheet so she would have enough time to schedule a meeting with the professor.

MAXIMIZE SUMMER & SEMESTER BREAKS

T he first instinct for students is to spend their summer and semester breaks relaxing and having fun. While there may be nothing wrong with doing this, successful students take advantage of these breaks from taking a full load of credits to prepare for the upcoming school year or to do things that will help them after college. If they plan it right, they can have fun and relax for part of the time while making the most of the rest of the time.

ENROLL IN SUMMER SCHOOL

Students who take summer school like this opportunity for several reasons.

- It can help them get ahead and possibly even graduate earlier than if they had not taken summer courses.

- The students could take the classes in the summer and then enroll in a lighter load during the school year while staying on track to graduate at the normal time. This is especially useful for students who know they will have to take demanding classes in the future.

➹ Since summer school sessions are shorter in duration, students who dread taking a particular class can take it in the summer and get it over with quickly.

Students who are planning on taking summer school should plan carefully, however, because only certain classes are offered in the summer. They should save these classes for summer.

Do an Internship

Students who participate in an internship can spend the summer building their resumes and exploring their proposed career tracks. They will build up some networking contacts and references for when they apply for a job after graduation. Internships have other benefits as well:

➹ They help students confirm whether they are making the right career and educational choices.

➹ They give students valuable insights to take back to the classroom.

➹ They allow students to make real-world connections to what they are learning in the classroom.

➹ They give students the motivation they need to successfully finish the last few semesters before graduation.

Volunteer

Colleges and universities typically have volunteer programs to help students find organizations to help. Volunteering can be done during the school year, during the summer, or during a semester or spring break. Some universities even offer volunteering vacations instead of the traditional spring break destinations for students.

Volunteering can help students learn more about their area of study, feel good about doing something good for other people, reach one or more of their goals, become more independent, and become more appreciative of everything they have. Volunteering is a valuable learning experience that students may not have the time for after they graduate and are holding down a job.

CASE STUDY: DAWN SCHNEIDER

Dawn Schneider is a junior political science major at the University of South Carolina Upstate in Spartanville, South Carolina.

Dawn's thoughts on the learning style:

The hardest thing about studying in college for me was getting adjusted to it. The workload I had in high school was much lighter than the workload I encountered when I came to college so I felt overwhelmed by it at first.

I didn't know where to begin. The biggest surprise for me when it came to studying in college was that as long as you're organized and stay motivated, it's not as hard as it seems at first.

Dawn's thoughts on distractions and balancing time:

Anything can pull me away from my studies if I don't want to study at the moment. I overcome this lack of motivation by either writing out a list of things that I have to finish or making one in my head and following it as closely as possible. Between activities I will allow myself short breaks to reward myself for each thing that I complete.

Dawn's thoughts on figuring out study tricks:

One trick I've found that helps me be a study successfully is the power of

CASE STUDY: DAWN SCHNEIDER

re-writing my notes before a test. Re-writing my notes, even if it's only once, helps me remember the material more easily than if I tried to memorize it by just looking at it.

Dawn's thoughts on challenges:

I think the biggest challenge for college students when it comes to maintaining good grades is staying focused despite all of the distractions that may come your way. You have to be as organized as possible. After all, you can't maintain good grades if you don't know when certain assignments are due or when your tests are!

EASE THE TRANSITION

Transitioning from high school or full-time employment into a full-time college student role can be a difficult transition. The independence, the varied schedules, and the new demands put on each student can be a difficult adjustment. Learning how to anticipate and deal with these transition issues can make the difference between just being a student and being a successful student.

ANTICIPATE THE LEARNING STYLE

Successful high school students can have a difficult time transitioning into the new learning style of college. In high school they thrived on contact with teachers, a solid schedule, study halls, and the relatively low workload. In college, students struggle because they have to start studying or figure out a new way to study. They also struggle with the concept that no one holds them accountable for what they do.

Successful students who transition to the new learning style examine their old study methods, learn new study methods, and explore the resources available to help them continue their success.

EASE THE FEARS

While they may not admit it, students can have a difficult time transitioning into college because they fear the unknown. Perhaps they have not been away from home before and have thrived on the comfort of their hometown and the familiarity of their classmates. College is a huge step and students do not know what to expect. They are not experienced in things they will now be responsible for such as laundry or cooking. Successful students have found ways to ease these transitions:

- **Successful students** go to freshman orientation meetings to learn about the university, learning tips for living on campus, understanding campus rules and regulations, and meeting new people.

- **Successful students** look for freshman transition meetings. These can cover a myriad of topics such as learning to deal with household chores like laundry, cooking, and cleaning as well as budgeting and time management.

- **Successful students** join a club or organization to meet new people in a social setting right away. This helps them find other students who are experiencing the same transition as well as students who have already been through it.

TRANSITIONING THE NON-TRADITIONAL STUDENT

Non-traditional students go through a transition process as well. Here are some tips to help them ease into college life:

- Non-traditional students may not live in residence halls on campus, so they may feel disconnected from the university as a whole. They can solve this by spending time on campus during the day; relaxing in the union and studying at the library are ways to connect with the campus.

- Non-traditional students may have to adjust from working full-time to having a mixed schedule of classes and free time. They struggle with using free time if their job was demanding all day long or with attending classes if their job included more independence. The way to solve this problem is to see each day as a work day from 8 a.m. until 5 p.m. and use that time for studying and classes.

- Non-traditional students may be lonely. This feeling can be alleviated by attending the non-traditional student orientation to meet other non-traditional students. Some universities also offer seminars for adult continuing education that can help non-traditional students overcome their transition struggles.

CASE STUDY: SHERYL BLAHNIK,

Sheryl Blahnik is the dean of academic support services at Richland Community College. She previously served as the dean of enrollment and retention services and as a student development and services counselor at Richland Community College.

Sheryl's thoughts on student adjustment:

Students struggle with learning to balance time, understanding the workload, and learning how to set priorities. The ultimate concern is learning how to use a computer and other basic technologies necessary for their coursework.

Sheryl's thoughts on student surprises:

The students here are surprised by their lack of computer skills and the amount of work they are expected to do. The biggest surprise can be that their family and friends see them moving ahead and this sometimes leads to interpersonal conflict.

CASE STUDY: SHERYL BLAHNIK,

Sheryl's thoughts on student distractions and advice:

In a non-residential setting there are many distractions. Students have full lives with full schedules long before they come to college. They are trying to fit in classes around everything they are doing. **Sheryl's thoughts on important study tips:**

Get help early in the semester if you are experiencing any concerns or self-doubt. Type notes, make flashcards, and study with small groups.

Sheryl's thoughts on memories:

I am 50 years old and I wish that we would have had the kind of technology available now when I was a student. I retyped my master's final paper eight times from start to finish. Today, students just make edits as they go. Life has become less complicated in some ways and more complex in others.

Sheryl's thoughts on student challenges:

The first challenge is to realize that they are only in competition with themselves for grades. They have to learn to be self-motivating, self-regulating, and disciplined students to be productive. Another big challenge is that some students do not feel confident that they can be successful

APPROACH THE PROFESSOR

It is unlikely that any successful student will graduate from college without having had to approach a professor outside class at least once. How they go about meeting with the professor can make or break the professor's opinion of the student.

SET UP A MEETING

The first thing a student needs to do when trying to meet with a professor is check the professor's office hours. Even though office hours are there for the professor to meet with students, it is best to try to set something up ahead of time just in case the professor has other meetings scheduled. This can be done with an e-mail or phone call to the his or her office.

There will be times when the student has a quick question for the professor and just stops by during office hours. This is acceptable, but it is best to not drop in during the last few minutes of the scheduled office hours. If the professor has to go to a meeting or a class immediately following office hours, he or she will not be able to give full attention to the question.

Prepare for the Meeting

After the meeting is set, it is important to prepare for the meeting. This includes making a list of questions and gathering all relevant material including class notes and the textbook. The student should also bring a notebook and pen to take notes.

Be Polite

There is nothing worse for a professor than a student entering his or her office and being disrespectful, unappreciative, blaming, or otherwise impolite. Students who are polite and respectful will be more likely to get a favorable response.

Keep Expectations in Check

Students who go see the professor expecting they will get exactly what they want when they want it will be disappointed. Just because a student goes in to contest a grade on an assignment or exam does not mean the professor is going to change that grade, even if the student believes they have good reason to request the change. Students should also not expect to get a direct answer from the professor. The professor may make suggestions or give hints toward the answer, but they want the student to continue thinking about the problem instead of having a solution handed to them.

Stay Open-Minded

Because some students spend so much time looking at the end point — finishing the paper, acing the exam, completing the semester, or even holding that degree in their hands — they start to have tunnel vision and forget there are multiple ways to do things and varied viewpoints to consider along the way. It is not unusual for a student to meet with a professor about a problem, misunderstanding, or a need for guidance with his or her mind set one way. It is the professor's job to help the student look at the issue from other perspectives, and if the student cannot widen his or her tunnel vision to see things differently, the meeting will likely end without making much progress.

For example, a student may be having difficulties finding information for a research project. They meet with the professor for suggestions and the professor simply says, "Try varying your search terms." To the student, this is no help because the answer is not what she was looking for. She wanted some specific locations or search terms to get her started. The professor, however, refuses to give this information to the student because part of the grade for the research paper depends on how well the student can use her resources to find the necessary information. The student then struggles through lists of search terms as one idea leads to another. The student later realizes the value in that lesson because, with practice, researching has become easy for her.

Successful students attend meetings with professors with an open mind so they can listen to and comprehend the suggestions the professor makes to help them, even if the suggestions do not seem helpful at the moment.

CONCLUSION

It is now time for the student to decide what type of student to be. They can be the student who does nothing but study all the time. They could also be the student who is struggling to keep up and forcing themselves to cram the night before exams because he or she has not yet taken the time to get organized and make a plan. If the student wants to get the most out of college, they strive to be the balanced student who knows how to study efficiently, have fun, and participate in activities.

This book is not the magic wand that will suddenly make studying so easy that the successful student will no longer need to work at being a successful student. No book can make a student succeed without their own motivation. Instead, this book provides students with the tools needed to become more effective; only they can ensure the tools are put to proper use. It is my hope that all students who read this book find at least a few nuggets of wisdom to help make their college careers more enjoyable by helping them carve out the time needed to do well in their classes and enjoy the journey.

Happy studying!

BIBLIOGRAPHY

Felder, Richard M., and Barabara A. Soloman, "Learning Styles and Strategies." **www.ncsu.edu.**

Jacobs, Lynn F. and Jeremy S. Hyman, *Professor's Guide to Getting Good Grades in College,* HarperCollins, New York, 2006.

Kingsbury, Alex, "Get in, show up, drop out: Trying to learn why so many college students fail to graduate," *U.S. News & World Report,* November 20, 2005.

Newport, Cal, *How to Become a Straight-A Student: The Unconventional Strategies Real College Students Use to Score High While Studying Less,* Broadway Books, New York, 2007.

Newport, Cal, *How to Win at College: Surprising Secrets for Success from the Country's Top Students,* Broadway Books, New York, 2005.

Pauk, Walter, *How to Study in College* 7th ed., Houghton Mifflin, New York, 2001.

Reynolds, Jean, *Succeeding in College: Study Skills and Strategies,* 2d ed., Prentice Hall, United States, 2002.

Van Blerkhom, Dianna L., *College Study Skills: Becoming a Strategic Learner* 5th ed., Thomson Wadsworth, United States, 2006.

AUTHOR DEDICATION & BIOGRAPHY

To Doug. *Because of you I am able to follow my heart and be the person I want to be. I love you.*

To Mom and Dad. *Thank you for giving me a love of reading, language and learning.*

To Teri, Adrienne, and Emily. *It is the memories of our college friendships that have made writing this book so entertaining.*

Susan Roubidoux is a former high school language arts teacher and has also developed study skills workshops for both the high school and collegiate levels. She has a Bachelor of Science, Secondary Education in English and Communication from the University of Wisconsin Oshkosh. She is currently a freelance writer in Winneconne, Wisconsin where she lives with her husband and three sons.

INDEX